I0190825

Commentary on the Epistle of FIRST JOHN

BY

Paul F. (Fred) Hall

FWB
Publications
The Rest is Less

Cover was from a painting by Valentin de Boulogne Born   3 January 1591 Coulommiers, France-Public Domain

To order additional copies of this book contact:

FWB Publications
Enchanted Acres
1006 Rayme Drive
Columbus, Ohio 43207
Ot www.amazon.com-978-1-940609-86-7

FWB

AN INTRODUCTION TO THE EPISTLE

In this epistle the loving heart of one who is genuinely concerned about the spiritual welfare of the people to whom he writes is clearly seen, an affection that is a reflection of one who has what has been called a "pastor's heart. He is concerned about anything that threatens their spiritual welfare, and he is concerned about their personal relationship with the God who loves them and who has provided salvation for them in the person of Jesus Christ.

It is a concern that is refreshing to us in this generation of the church age, for we see so little of it evidenced among many who are the "so-called spiritual leaders of God's people. If anything, a study of this marvelous epistle should cause us to return to a time of genuine concern for others, and a return to a New Testament kind of fellowship among believers.

As our study progresses into this short epistle we will notice several words that occur over and over again. For instance, the word "know," or some derivative of that word, occurs over thirty times in the epistle. Obviously, the writer was concerned that the people who read this book would have some experiential knowledge of the Lord and of spiritual matters.

Another word that is very prominent is "love." This word occurs over thirty times as well, and is used in the epistle as a sort of "test" to determine one's relationship with God and with man. The frequent occurrence of these words and other similar ones leads us to the conclusion that a major theme of the epistle is the assurance of salvation for those who have trusted in the Lord Jesus Christ for forgiveness of sin.

This theme is of vital importance to the spiritual welfare of believers in any age.

THE AUTHOR AND AUTHENTICITY OF THE EPISTLE

The epistle has, by tradition and strong evidence, been attributed to the Apostle John. The evidence for the Johannine authorship falls mainly into two parts: (1) the external evidence of the historical acceptance of the book as being from John, and (2) the internal evidence of the book which compares closely with the language and manner of the Gospel of John.

(1) THE EXTERNAL EVIDENCE: Many, if not all, of the early church fathers quoted the epistle of First John as having the authority of Scripture. Among them Polycarp, Eusebius, Irenaeus, Clement of Alexandria, Tertullius, Cyprian, and Origen (Thiessen, 307). Perhaps the best of the evidence comes from a first century preacher named Papias (about 125 A.D.) who quoted from the epistle regularly (Kistemaker, 195), and who Irenaeus (about 185 A.D.) identifies as a "hearer" of John's preaching(Kistemaker, 196). Since John lived up until the time of the emperor Trajan (98-117 A.D.) it is entirely possible that Papias was, indeed, one

of those who heard him speak, and because of his own experience accepted John's writings as being Scripture.

Further external evidence is seen from the third century preachers such as Clement of Alexandria, Origen, Tertullius, and Dionysius who referred to the epistles of John separately from his Gospel (Kistemaker, 196), and who considered them as Scripture on an equal basis with the Gospel.

It is clear from the external evidence contained in the testimony of the early fathers that they believed the epistle was authored by John the Apostle (Burdick, 12).

(2)THE INTERNAL EVIDENCE: Although the name of John is not mentioned within the text of the epistle, it is clear from the manner of writing and the language used that it is of Johannine origin (Thiessen, 307). For instance, the writer represents himself as being an eyewitness of Christ, having seen and heard everything about which he is writing (1:1-4; 4:14). John's closeness with Jesus, being one of his disciples and being present throughout His earthly ministry, certainly qualified him as the eyewitness who penned these words (Gromacki, 368).

In addition, the early fathers who quoted him were certainly familiar enough with his language and emphasis as to make him easily identifiable as the author of the epistle.

There are great similarities in the epistle with the words of the Gospel which give evidence that they were penned by the same person: Compare 1 John 1:4 with John 16:24 to see similar expression concerning the "complete joy" of the believer; 1 John 2:11 with John 12:35 to see similar references to the person who walks in "darkness;" and finally, 1 John 3:23 with John 13:34 to see the similarity of the commandment to "love one another."

These similarities, and many others, point to the shared authorship of both the Gospel and the epistle. The few objections to Johannine authorship of the epistle come from liberal scholars who identify the "Johannine School" of writers who shared the same philosophy as John and penned the epistle under his inspiration (Kistemaker, 201), but these objections are not really serious enough to be accepted as evidence against the Johannine authorship of the epistle.

THE OCCASION AND DATE OF THE EPISTLE

Although the epistle does not mention any particular church or churches as being the object of John's exhortations, It is generally accepted by many that the churches for which these writings were originally intended were the churches of Asia Minor mentioned in the book of Revelation: Smyrna, Pergamos, Thyatira, Sardis, Philadelphia, Laodicea, and Ephesus (Thiessen, 308), John made his home in Ephesus and had a special concern for these surrounding churches (Gromacki, 370). His special concern for the problems these churches faced occasioned the writing of the epistle.

The churches for whom this epistle was intended had problems in two areas: the problems from within the family of believers, and the threat from without contained in the false philosophies of the day.

THE PROBLEMS FROM WITHIN: From an examination of the epistle itself we find some serious problems in the lives of the believers.

(1) Many of them lacked sincere love for others. John warned them against harboring "hate" for a brother in 2:7-11.
(2) They had problems with worldliness, being affected by the sinfulness of those around them. John warns them not to love this world of sinful things in 2:15-17.

(3) Many of them lacked a real concern about those about them who had real needs, thus failing to evidence a genuine Christian love for their brethren, 3:17-24.

(4) There was a lack of assurance of salvation among many. John writes to encourage these and to help them to know about their salvation, 5:13.

THE PROBLEMS FROM WITHOUT: As if the problems within the congregation were not enough, these believers were also in danger of being influenced by the teachings of the Gnostics, the chief advocate of which was a man named Cerinthus (Barker,

295). Cerinthus was educated in Egypt (Thiessen, 309) and was quite influential in proclaiming the heresy of the Gnostics. The main teachings which John sought to neutralize in the minds of the believers concerned those about the person of Christ. These teachings were:

1.   That Jesus was born like all others of a human mother and father, Joseph and Mary, and therefore denied the Virgin Birth.

2.   That Jesus and Christ were separate; Christ being a spirit and Jesus being a sinful human form. Thus, they denied that Jesus could have.been God in the flesh.

3.   That the spirit Christ descended on Jesus at His baptism but departed from Him prior to His death. They denied that Christ the spirit could suffer at all since He did not possess a human body. Prior to the death of Jesus the spirit Christ returned to the "fullness of the Father. This teaching effectively does away with the atonement (Kistemaker, 213, 214).

These threats from without went to the very heart of the Gospel and, with good reason, gave some alarm to John. If these teachings were to be accepted by the believers of that day their basis for salvation would be eliminated and they would have become apostate in their faith.

Most scholars agree that both the Gospel of John and this epistle were written fairly close together in terms of timing. The dates most agree upon are between 85 and 90 A.D. (Thiessen, 310, and Gromacki, 370). Thiessen reasons that the destruction of Jerusalem occurred around 70 A.D. which brought about a wide dispersion of believers in that day. John lived until the time of Trajan (about 98 A.D.), so the writing would have to have been after the dispersion and before the 98 A.D. date. Thus, the most reasonable timing for the epistle would be the stated dates of 85-90 A.D.

THE PURPOSE OF THE EPISTLE

Apart from the concerns already mentioned (the Gnostic threat from without and the spiritual problems from within), John states clearly the purposes for which he wrote this epistle: In 1:4 his purpose is that their "joy may be full." In 2:1 his purpose is that they know what to do about their sin problem.

The ideal is that they never sin. But, if they sin, they have an "advocate in Jesus.

1. 1 In 2:26 his purpose is to warn the believers against those who would "seduce" them into believing lies.

2. In 5:13 his purpose is to give assurance to those who were suffering some doubt about their salvation. He wanted them to have a certain

knowledge of the forgiveness that Jesus had provided them when they believed in Him.

THE STRUCTURE AND OUTLINE OF THE EPISTLE

This epistle presents some problems in its structure, for it seems to move from one subject to another, then return again later on to the same subject. Some have called these movements "cycles" because of their seemingly circular structure (Burdick, 14, 15). John's presentation is basically a pastor's concern for the people whom he loves. This outline will be based on that pastoral concern which John displays for all people, but most especially for those under his pastoral care.

The Introduction - Establishing the Premise of the Epistle (1:1-4)

- The Life that is Real (1:1,2)

- The Fellowship that is Divine (1:3)

- The Joy that Is Full (1:4)

Walking In the Light of God (1:5-2:27)

- By confession of sin (1:5-2:2)

- By obedience to God's commands (2:3-11)

- By avoiding involvement with the world system (2:12-17)

- By rejecting the teaching of the anti-Christ's (2:18-28)

Experiencing the Righteousness of God (2:29-4:6)

- By knowing Christ, Who is the righteousness of believers (2:29-3:10)

- By expressing the love of Christ, Who loved us first (3:11-18)

- By confidently trusting in the truth of God (3:19-24)

- By rejecting completely the spirit of error proclaimed by the false prophets (4:1-6)

Manifesting the Love of God (4:7-5:12)
- By loving others as God loved us (4:7-21)

- By loving God with our total being (5:1-12)

The Epilogue: The Assurance of Salvation (5:13-21)

COMMENTARY

The Introduction
Establishing the Premise of the Epistle (1:1-4)

When we understand the position of one who is speaking or writing to us (modernvernacular - "where they are coming from")we then can understand more clearly what he is saying. John announces from the very beginning of the epistle exactly what his position is as it relates to Christ, and as it relates to those who have opposed him in hisministry.

His premise is that he believes in a Christ who is eternally existent; a Christ who has been manifested to men; and a Christ with whom he is personally acquainted.

As he proceeds through the epistle he will not waver from that position nor compromise his personal convictions concerning the person of Jesus Christ.

A. The Life that is Real (1:1,2)

That which was from the beginning, which we have heard,

which we have seen with our eyes, which we have looked upon, and our hands have handled, of the Word of life;

"(For the life was manifested, and we have seen it, and bear witness, and shew unto you that eternal life, which was with the Father, and was manifested unto us.)"

The first four verses of the epistle constitute the introduction to the epistle and make up one long sentence.

The first verse is made up of relative clauses which find their action verb in verse 3 where John says he will "declare" to his readers. The second verse is a parenthetic expansion on the real subject of the introduction, the "Word of life" who is Jesus Christ.

There are three basic things that John wants to establish about Jesus Christ here: (1)that he existed eternally - he was "from the beginning;" (2)that he was real in the sense that he had a body that could both be seen and touched; and (3)that through him man could receive the "Word" that could bestow life. This was in contrast to that which was being pro-claimed by the Gnostics of his day that (1)Jesus was just a man like all other men and had only a human existence; (2) God could not occupy human bodies since flesh and spirit were opposites and could not occupy the same space at the same time; and (3)man was given life through some special and secret "knowledge" and not from God himself. (The Gnostic of the New Testament time believed if he had this special and secret "knowledge" at the time of his death, he would float free among the demons of the after-life without harm, finally to be reunited with the Creation Deity. (Douglas, 417). The aim of the Gnostic, therefore, was to find that special and secret knowledge and not trust his final destiny to a redeemer.)

There are also some things which John wants to establish about himself in these short verses: (1)He wants to establish his RIGHT to speak about this "real" Christ. He was present with him and "heard" him speak, saw him with his own eyes, and "looked" upon him, even going so far as being able to touch him with his hands. (2)He wants to establish that, because of his own personal experience with Jesus Christ, he is able to give authoritative explanation of Christ's Person and work among men. (3)He clearly wants to establish his absolute opposition to the teachings of the Gnostics, and his purpose to proclaim the truth about Jesus Christ to his readers.

We can compare John 1:1-14 to see what he meant when he proclaims at the very start of the epistle he is declaring the truth about "that which was from the beginning." By that he is saying that Jesus Christ shares with God the Father eternal existence, and thus is co-equal with the Father. Only One who is divine can be eternally existent, and this eternal existence carries with it the meaning of: (1)incarnation-that God became a man in the person of Christ (John 1:1); (2)creation- that Jesus was present and participated with the Father in the creation of all things (John 1:3); (3) salvation - Jesus is the personification and source of life for all men (John 1:4,12); and (4) grace and truth expressed through the life and teachings of Jesus. John would declare "that which we have heard" as it relates to the teachings of Christ. His was not a truth that originated within his own mind, or within the confines of his own prejudices.

Rather, what John would declare to his readers was truth learned sitting at the feet of Jesus and walking by his side as he ministered to the people who came into contact with him. What he had heard from Jesus had not just entered his mind - it had also entered his heart and had changed him completely. It was this life-changing truth, taught by Christ himself, which John so eagerly sought to impart to the people whom he loved.

The next two statements are inter-related and progressive in what John is declaring. First he says he will declare that "which we have seen with our eyes." The word "seen" comes from the Greek root word "Horao" which refers to actual physical sight. It is the act of seeing something or someone simply as an object. In fact John explains further that he had seen "with our eyes," indicating that he had been in the presence of Christ and had "seen" him physically as a real object. His second statement is progressive. He proceeds from seeing Christ as an object to "looking" or "gazing" upon him. This is a different Greek form from "Horao." The word here is from the Greek root word "Theaomai" which means to "see with admiration, desire, or regard" (Vine, 337). William Barclay says of this word that it is a "steadfast, searching gaze which seeks to discover something of the mystery of Christ" (Barclay, 23), Not only did John "see" Christ, but he also "gazed" upon him long enough and sincerely enough to discover something about Jesus that changed his life, The change which he experienced by being in contact with the "real" Christ had given a new direction to his entire being.

John had come in touch with this "real" Christ, not only with his physical eyes and his mind, but he had also "handled" him. Perhaps he is remembering that appearance of the resurrected Christ when Thomas was invited to touch the wounds to make sure that Jesus was not a ghost but a real, living person (John 20:26-29), The "spirit Christ" of the Gnostics could not be handled and touched, but the "real" Christ could, and John had experienced that wonderful sensation.

All of these statements are about the "Word of life," whom John wishes to proclaim to his readers. This is the "Word" which he proclaimed in the Gospel which bears his name. Jesus is the "Logos" of God, the "declaration" of God in the flesh.

Jesus appearance among men in the flesh was not just a manifestation of a body, but God's way of communicating with man his concern and love for a lost humanity. In Christ we are able to witness all the attributes of a Holy God, and we are able to understand from the sacrifice of Jesus the extent to which God was willing to go to redeem sinful man to himself.

The word "Logos" in the Greek meant "speech or revelation as the clarification or explanation of something" (TDNT,506)and as it was applied to Christ it meant that he was the revelation and clarification of God, being co-equal with the Father.

In other words, Jesus revealed and clarified God to man in doing so, Jesus became, in bodily form, all that was contained in the law of God, for in him "God's word is not just transmitted but enacted" (TDNT,514).

The parenthetical verse 2 is simply an expansion upon what John has already said in verse 1. He states simply that this "Word of life" has been manifested to man, and that he has been a witness of that manifestation. He states further that he wants to communicate to his readers the "eternal life" which Jesus Christ represents, and make sure that they know he was with the Father, but has now been revealed unto man. This is the life that is "real" - not the figment of someone's imagination, but that which all men can know for a certainty.

B. The Fellowship that is Divine (1:3)

"That which we have seen and heard declare we unto you, that ye also may have fellowship with us: and truly our fellowship is with the Father, and with his Son Jesus Christ."

The whole purpose of declaring the truths about Christ which John had "seen" and "heard was so that the believers to whom he had addressed this epistle might share a fellowship with each other, and in turn might share that fellowship with the Father and the Son. Just as the key word in vv. 1, 2 was life, the key word here in v. 3 is the word "fellowship." The word fellowship comes from the Greek word "Koinonia" which means a "communion, fellowship, sharing in common" (Vine,90). The First Century church consisted of people from varying cultures and social position. There were both Jew and Gentile believers in the church, very different in concept and practice of their daily life, and yet all of these were joined together in one, sharing a common bond. That common bond was not in their cultural background, education, religious upbringing, or any other human element.

Rather the bond of their fellowship was in a person, Jesus Christ. John declared the truth about Jesus Christ in order for all men to place faith in him and be brought into this wonderful and divine fellowship. This fellowship could not be shared apart from Jesus Christ and the truth which he declared and taught. Thus, the purpose of John's declarations was to bring his readers into this common fellowship of a shared salvation based on faith in Christ.

But this fellowship is not just on a human level. Our shared faith in Christ raises believers to a higher level of fellowship - a level which includes the Father and the Son. The basis of this fellowship is faith, and no person can be admitted into it apart from a genuine faith in Jesus Christ as personal Saviour. But what a fellowship this is! What a glory and privilege it is for the believer to be able to share a part of himself with the Father and the Son, and for the Father and the Son to share a part of themselves with the believer.

C. The Joy that is Full (1:4)

"And these things write we unto you, that your joy may be full."

Here is one of the stated purposes of John in writing this epistle. Statements like this one help us to know that John had a pastor's heart, one that was concerned about the spiritual welfare of people. He knew there was no joy in sin, for the "wages of sin is death" (Romans 3:23). He knew there was no joy in what the Gnostics were teaching, for theirs was a philosophy based on man and his abilities, and at best man is unreliable.

The joy for the believer would be obtained through faith in Christ, the one who was being proclaimed by John in the verses preceding (vv. 1-3). He would be their source of joy, their reason for rejoicing. And this joy would be "full" - the meaning here is "complete," lacking nothing (Vine, 136).

Summary (1:1-4)

John wastes no time in establishing his basic premise: that Jesus as the Christ has always existed with the Father, but has now been revealed unto men to declare how God feels about mankind; that Jesus is God in the flesh and that by trusting in him by faith man can not only share a common bond with other men, but can be raised to a level of sharing fellowship with the Father and the Son. The reason for John's declaration is so that the people about whom he is concerned can have a joy that is full and complete, not lacking in anything that would satisfy the soul and enrich the spirit of man.

Practical Teaching and Preaching Applications

There is an abundance of material here to use as a basis for proclaiming the truth in this generation. The Gnostic heresy has not disappeared from our midst at all. It is here, and we are surrounded by it, although it may take upon itself different names, and even deny that is a Gnostic heresy. But the root of the heresy of Gnosticism lies in the pride of man and his constant effort to save himself. There are those all around us who proclaim that they have some "secret" knowledge that the Christian does not have. The Mormons emphasize that they have "another revelation of Jesus Christ" in their Book of Mormon, and by that statement deny the truthfulness and reliability of the written word of God, the Bible.

A meaningful message could be organized around the Person of Christ as John declares him here:

I.   Christ the Eternal One (1:1)- as the Eternal Christ

he shares oneness with the Father, and therefore shares the Father's attributes: Omniscience, omnipresence, omnipotence, etc. This is a source of comfort to all those who need to trust in One who not only wants to help, but who possesses the power to help.

II. Christ the Revealed One (1:2) - God can be discovered through knowing Christ. He is the "revealer" of God because he is the "Word of life." God does not want to be a mystery to anyone, but wants to make himself known, and this he has done through his Son Jesus Christ.

III. Christ the Sharing One (1:3,4)- Jesus not only gave himself to die on the cross, but he also "indwells" the believer, sharing himself for the purpose of assuring, guiding, empowering, and speaking through the believer. We can truly sing from our hearts, "What a fellowship, what a joy divine!"

There can also be a wonderful emphasis here on the "Joy" of the believer. One of John's purposes in writing this epistle was to bring full and complete joy to the believer's heart. The life of the believer should be filled with joy every day, and can be when he fully understands the nature of Christ - that he is the Word of life - and the Person of Christ - that he is God come in the flesh to reveal to man just how much God loves him.

This joy comes from personal experience, not from some philosophical statement. For anyone to obtain the "joy" of the

Lord it is necessary to "know" the Lord Jesus in the same way John knew him. A person must not only "see" him as an object (this is the way that the majority of people understand Christ), but he must also "gaze" upon him with admiration and trust to discover who Christ is and what he wants to do for the person. Herein lies the nature of the New Birth (John 3:3, 5) which is an absolute necessity for the forgiveness of sins and the "creating anew" of the sinner (2Corinthians 5:17).

I. Walking In the Light of God (1:5-2:27)

Nothing is more important to John than that his people walk in the light of God. Their conduct of life is a reflection of their obedience to, and faith in, the Lord Jesus Christ. His pastor's heart is concerned about the outward testimony of professing believers, and also the inward joy of those will so live.

A.   By Confession of Sin (1:5-2:2)

(1)   There is no darkness (sin) in God (1:5)

"This then is the message which we have heard of him, and declare unto you, that God is light, and in him is no darkness at all."

John has a message to deliver to his people, a message that comes from his own personal experience with the Lord Jesus Christ as he has already recounted in vv. 1-4. This message is one which does not come from himself, but from 'the Lord Jesus Christ who told it to him. John states plainly that this message was "heard of him." It is then imperative that he declare this divine message with accuracy and truthfulness.

The message concerns the very nature of God and is in two parts:

He states that "God is light" - this is the positive side of the message; and (2)he states that there is no "darkness" in him "at all" - this is the negative side of the message, God IS light, God IS NOT darkness. This goes to the very nature of God.

"God is light" - John is not saying that God "gives off" light, or even that he is the "source" of light.   He is saying that God is the personification of light, the kind of light that infers infinite holiness, absolute purity, and perfect righteousness. This is his nature, it is what God is, a statement about his mode of existence. John uses this "light" to describe the nature and work of Jesus in his Gospel (ref.:John 1:4, 5, 9; 3:19; 8:12; 9:5; 12:35, 36, 46).

Since this is the nature of God, and this nature cannot be compromised, the only way for men to have fellowship with him is to "walk in the light as he is in the light" (v.7), since to do otherwise would be in opposition to his holiness, purity, and righteousness.

"In him is no darkness at all" - this is the negative side of the description of the nature of God in relation to sin. God IS NOT darkness - there is nothing in him that has anything at all to do with sin and wickedness. Paul understood this truth when he asked, "What communion has light with darkness?"

(2) Corinthians 6:14). John emphasizes this truth when he made the statement adding another negative to it. The Amplified Version translates the last phrase this way, "there is no darkness in him at all- no, not in any way." For any darkness to be in God would be to detract from his holy nature and thus violate his stated character of light. Lenski has the right idea when he states, "there is absolutely no darkness in God, not even one small shadow that might dim his truth, righteousness, and holiness" (Lenski, 385).

How then is it possible, then, for sinful man to have fellowship with such a God who is absolutely holy, pure, and righteous? John now proceeds to answer that all-important question.

2. The possibility of fellowship with the God of light (1:6, 7)

"If we say that we have fellowship with him, and walk in darkness, we lie, and do not the truth:

"But if we walk in the light, as he is in the light, we have fellowship one with another, and the blood of Jesus Christ his Son cleanseth us from all sin."

John here speaks of two kinds of people: (a)those who

"say" they have fellowship with the Lord Jesus, but do not present any corroborating evidence by their changed life style; and (b) those who evidence their changed life style by the way they "walk in the light." It is one thing to "say" one is having fellowship with God, and quite another to prove that fellowship by walking as Jesus walked.

He is saying that even if "we" (you and I) do not live up to our profession it is an empty statement, and meaningless. Perhaps he had someone in mind when he spoke these words about those who only "claimed" to have fellowship with the Lord. It could have been the Gnostics who claimed some kind of relationship with God, 'but one based on a different foundation than the Gospel of Jesus Christ. Perhaps he knew of some in the church who "professed a better game than they actually played. Whatever the case, v. 6 plainly describes those who say one thing, but by their lives contradict what they say, He is very plain in what he calls them- he says that they are "liars!"

Now a liar is someone who knows better. A liar purposely speaks falsely to hide the real truth. He is not walking openly, but secretly; and he is not living up to a truth known to him but rather he is violating that truth in every way, knowingly. That is what makes the liar's sin so much more damning - he knows differently and yet continues to speak falsely about his condition before God.

Now the second type of person here mentioned is the one who "walks in the light as he is in the light." What does it mean to "walk in the light?" It means to walk in the open, revealing oneself especially to God, but also to men. It is an open confession of one's sinful state, but a testimony that God has forgiven the sins that once dominated the life. It means that one is openly walking with God every day, unashamed of that Holy Communion, and speaking every day of the goodness of the Lord. It means also, that the believer has agreed to the standard of holiness, righteousness, and purity set by the Saviour and is trying to live by that standard every day. The pattern for this "walk" for the believer is the Lord himself.

John says, "as he is in the light"- that is where the inspiration for the walk is found. We found out in v. 5 that there is no darkness at all in God, nothing in him that would dim his holiness, righteousness, and purity. So then, God must be not only the personification of light, but also he is "in" the light. That is where he is found, and if the believer would share fellowship with him he must go where he is, walk where he walks, and share in his nature. Again Lenski says, "To walk in the light is above all to believe the light, the truth, and then also to obey it in word and in deed." (Lenski, 388).

Now we come to the two things that result from our "walking in the light" in perfect obedience to God's truth - (a)we have fellowship with one another, and (b)the blood of Jesus Christ cleanses us from all sin.

3. We have fellowship with one another.

The word fellowship indicates a "sharing" or a communion" that is enjoyed by the family of believers. Because we are living according to the standards of the Lord himself we have a special love for each other, the same kind of love that Jesus had for us, and continues to have for us daily. This loving fellowship is the sign that we are truly the sons of God (John 13:35) and have been changed from the selfish and egocentric people that we were to those who reach out to others in the Name of Jesus Christ.

(a)   The blood of Jesus Christ cleanses us from sin.

Since it would be impossible for anyone to have fellowship with the Lord while walking in darkness, God has provided through the sacrifice of Jesus on the cross for that darkness to be taken away. When our sins have been forgiven through the application of the blood of Jesus then we may continue our walk uninterrupted by the darkness. The word for "cleanseth" here is the Greek "catharizei" which means to "make clean from defilement" (Vine,195).The blood of Jesus is the cleansing agent whereby all the filth of sin that would rob us of fellowship with the God who is light is completely washed away.

The word for cleansing here is in the present tense, indicating a continuous action taking place. The verse could be read as follows: "and the blood of Jesus Christ his Son CONTINUES TO CLEANSE us from all sin."

Glenn Barker wrote of this marvelous truth, "The present Tense of the verb stresses Christ's work as an ongoing provision against present and future contingencies. Without it enduring fellowship would be impossible, for the guilt resulting from sin destroys fellowship." (Barker, 311). As the believer walks in the light of the Lord there is a spiritual growth constantly taking place that causes one to love other believers and to be sensitive to one's own personal state before God. The constant and continuous cleansing of the blood of Jesus Christ makes it possible for the believer to stay in the pathway of light and in perfect fellowship with God through the Lord Jesus Christ.

(b) The Confession that is necessary (1:8-10)

"If we say that we have no sin, we deceive ourselves, and the truth is not in us.

"If we confess our sins, he is faithful and just to forgive us our sins, and to cleanse us from all unrighteousness.

"If we say that we have not sinned, we make him a liar, and his word is not in us."

In this passage we find John speaking of a world of denial on the part of those who have sinned, and at the same time a merciful forgiveness for those who will claim it through confession of sin and trusting in Jesus Christ. It is the desire of John that men repent of their sins rather than continue in their denial. We will consider these verses according to their subject matter rather than according to their numbered order: the two denials of sin, vv. 8, 10, then the promise of forgiveness, v. 9.

The first denial, "If we say that we have no sin," speaks to the sin principle in all men. It is a denial of one's sinful nature, that urge to sin which is in every man, "Sin is motivated by a human impulse that is present in all of us, so that in thousands of variations we will all be tempted similarly and sin similarly. (TDNT,46), There were those in John's day who denied that man was capable of a sinful nature. "John is referring to the Gnostic subtlety that sin was a matter of the flesh and did not touch or defile the spirit" (Stott,77). In its simplest form it is really a claim to sinless perfection, or even an equality with God, thus no accountability for sin in the life. There are many, like the Gnostics, who believe that since they have supposedly placed their faith in Christ they may go on and sin as much as they desire. But John is very clear in pointing out the two results of such thinking:

1. We deceive ourselves - There is nothing so pitiful than self-deception in the matter of sin. That which is so obvious, even to the casual observer, is seemingly hidden from the eyes and understanding of the one committing the sin. When the denial is made that one does not even have the urge to sin, therefore no guilt for that which is committed in his life, the deception is limited to the one who is saying it, for no one else - not friend, family, or God – is deceived in such a way. It is a pitiable state because the one so deceived cannot be moved to do anything about their guilt, and most surely will die without God because of their self-deception.

2. "The truth is not in us — Because of the denial No truth can abide in the heart of the self-deceived, The truth of the Scriptures is that ALL have this basic urge to sin: Romans 5:12; 3:23.   Since the Scriptures are the truth which God calls upon us to believe, to deny what the Scriptures teach about the urge and nature of sin is to reject truth. Where rejection is truth cannot abide.

The second denial, "If we say that we have not sinned," speaks to the denial of acts of unrighteousness, the outward product of the inner urge to sin. This denial is so blatant that the average Christian is shocked by it. It seems so unreal to think that someone would actually deny any acts of sin in their life, and yet John realizes that some have already denied such wickedness. The two results of such a denial are:

1. "We make him a liar — In the light of God's Word that plainly teaches that all men have sinned, and that there is "none righteous, no not one   (Romans 3:10), to say that one has not committed acts of sin is to say that God is a liar. How bold Satan makes those who are in his control. He convinces those that they not are without the urge to sin, but that they have never committed acts of sin. They have deceived themselves, thus plunging themselves into a dangerous ignorance, and they have called God a liar, estranging themselves from the only one who could help them out of their deception.

"His word is not in us" - If God is thus labeled a liar how can His Word be "in us?" Not only is God rejected, but the Word which He has spoken is also rejected, and the one guilty of such rejection is plunged into a spiritual darkness that will take a miracle to dispel. That miracle is to be found only in the offer of God found in v. 9. The foundation of the salvation of the believer lies in admitting and confessing his sins before God. Only through this means can God be able to forgive the sins and-change the state of the one confessing from being condemned to be saved. Verse 9 is proclaiming this divine condition to our forgiveness and salvation.

2. "If we confess our sins" - The word translated "confess" here means simply to "say the same thing, admit, declare" (Vine, 224) concerning our sins. We "say the same thing" as God says about them. In essence, when God says, "All have sinned" (Romans 3:23), then we reply, "Yes, Lord, that is me. I am one of those who have sinned." John is saying that when it comes to sin excuses and self-justification will not bring deliverance from guilt. Only an open hearted, sincere confession to God, admitting guilt and even specific acts of sin, will wipe out the past before God, and ensure that the future can be lived in the very presence of God through the forgiveness of Jesus Christ.

3. "He is faithful and just" - This is just another way of saying that Jesus can be relied upon to keep His promises, to do what He has said He would in regard to forgiveness. We may have

tried to deceive ourselves, but God has certainly not deceived us, for everything He has promised He will do.

The believer can come to Jesus with complete confidence because He is "faithful" to His own Word, and because He is "just" in His dealings with all who come to Him. "to forgive us our sins" - In this act of God our sins are "sent away" (Vine, 122) and therefore remembered no more against us. This action on God's part is prompted by the believer's confession of sins and faith in Jesus Christ as the great sin-bearer. In other words the guilt of sin is removed absolutely, therefore the believer can have perfect and unhindered fellowship with God.

4. and to cleanse us from all unrighteousness" - Again the word "cleanse" is used as it was in v. 7, and again it is in the present tense, indicating a continuous action taking place. Not only will Jesus forget us of our sins, but He will "continue to cleanse" us of "all unrighteousness." The Amplified Version defines this unrighteousness as "everything not in conformity to his will in purpose, thought, and action" (Amplified, 907).

The greatest blessing comes from a simple confession of all the sin one has committed, and a simple admission that the weakness in sinning comes from a basic nature in us that is corrupt and constantly weak in yielding to temptations. When we admit our need of help, and our need of forgiveness because of sin-guiltiness, then God, as the loving Father He is, is willing to forgive our guilt and keep on cleansing us as we walk with Him every day.

(4) A Pastoral Concern About Sin (2:1, 2)

"My little children, these things write I unto you, that ye sin not. And if any man sin, we have an advocate with the Father, Jesus Christ the righteous:

"And he is the propitiation for our sins: and not for ours only, but also for the sins of the whole world."

As we read these verses we can hear the Pastor's heart of John expressing his sincere concern about the spiritual welfare of the people whom God had given him. Such warm, fatherly affection is an indication of how personal his relationship was, and how high regard the people felt for him. They knew him by the affection he displayed for them. Perhaps that is the reason why it was not necessary for John to call himself by name in this epistle.

He wants them to know that even though they may weaken and sin in their lives, through ignorance, neglect, or weakness in yielding to temptation, there is still forgiveness possible for those who come to Christ. These two verses really tell the believer what he should do about sin, and how to escape the judgment for sin by coming to the One who really cares about him and can help him.

The literal rendition of the phrase "that ye sin not" is "that ye may not sin." (Berry, 609). John is stating the ideal. He is writing these things to them in order to warn them against sinning. He is spelling out the awful consequences of doing so, and trying to show them that sin will rob them of fellowship with God and with each other.

But at the same time John is showing the practical reality of the weakness of human nature, so he says to them, "And if any man sin•." He admits that although the ideal is that believers would not sin, at the same time believers do sin, either through ignorance, weakness, or even on purpose.

Admitting this practical reality John then gives to the believer the good news about how to overcome this sinning.

1.   When the believer sins, "We have an ADVOCATE with the Father, Jesus Christ the righteous." Jesus is the advocate for the believer. The word translated "advocate" is the Greek "paraklyton" which means "one who comes alongside, one who appears on another's behalf, a mediator, a helper." (Palmer, 36). Some have likened the advocate to the modern day lawyer who pleads the case of his client before the judge and jury. He stands between the accused and the judge and asks for consideration of mercy or justice in the matter before the court. Jesus, then, is the One who stands between the sinner and the judge of all men, and pleads our case before Him. What a glorious truth for the believer!   Just think - when the believer sins he is not immediately cast away from God and left alone in his

transgression; there is One who comes alongside of him to sustain him, to plead for him, to love him, and to help him to the place of forgiveness and restoration.

2. Not only is Jesus our Advocate, but He is also our

PROPITIATION. This word is also used in 4:10 referring to the expression of love the Father has for us in sending Jesus to be our PROPITIATION. The Greek word for "propitiation" is "hilasmos" which signifies "an expiation, a means whereby sin is covered and remitted." (Vine, 224). To understand the full meaning, however, we must go back to the Old Testament and the sacrificial system. The various offerings for sin were required to be blood offerings. The reason for this was that man had sinned and therefore forfeited his life and the only thing that could restore that life was the blood. This principle is laid down in Leviticus 17:11 - "For the life of the flesh is in the blood: and I have given it to you upon the altar to make an ATONEMENT for your souls: for it is the blood that maketh an ATONEMENT for the soul. Only the blood of the sacrifice could bring back again the life of the sinner, for the life is in the blood.

The blood of the sacrifice was a covering (Hebrew "kopher" used in connection with the mercy-seat - Vine, 223) sprinkled upon the mercy seat by the high priest. By this covering of blood God's judgment was forestalled for a season. The work of the cross is the work of restoring to mankind the life that has been lost through sin. Jesus is the One who sheds the blood that becomes the covering for the sinner. Since His blood is divine there is no further need of other blood sacrifices for the sinner. When the blood of Jesus is applied to the sinner's heart, God no longer sees the sinner and his sin, but He sees the blood of Jesus covering the guilt and restoring true life to the believer.

There is another meaning to the word PROPITIATION which Barclay so ably points out. It is the work of appeasing the anger God feels toward sin and the sinner. Referring to the verb form of the word, "hilaskesthai," he says, "When it is used with a man. It means to placate or pacify someone who has been injured or offended," (Barclay, 39). When man sins he offends a holy God who has already pronounced His sentence upon the sinner- "the wages of sin is death" (Romans 6:23) - and in order for forgiveness to be obtained that anger against sin on the part of God must be placated or appeased. When that has been done, then the believer can enter into perfect fellowship with God through the blood of Jesus Christ.

The important thing for the believer to remember is that his forgiveness and restoration is found in the work of Jesus Christ and not in some self-sufficient act of piety. Salvation is in a Person, not in a religion or a form. The Person and work of Jesus Christ is the Father's provision for all who sin, and forgiveness and right standing before a holy God can only be found in Him. John is deeply concerned that the people to whom he addresses this epistle will not be defeated by the sin they will commit because of their human frame, but will find victory in putting themselves by faith into the able hands of their Advocate and Propitiation,

Commentary on the Epistle of FIRST JOHN

Jesus Christ the righteous. John makes one more point in his pastoral concern for others The Person and work of Jesus is not only for the particular people to whom he addresses this epistle, but also for the multitudes of people in the whole world who sin. His is a universal concern, as the concern should be in the hearts of all believers. John expressed this universal concern in what it probably the most familiar text in the Bible, John 3:16 - "For God so love the WORLD, that he gave his only begotten Son, that WHOSOEVER believeth in him should not perish, but have everlasting life. "The blood of Jesus is sufficient to cover the sins of the whole world, and nothing would please Him more than if every man, woman, and child in the world would accept His offered salvation. The problem is, even though salvation in Christ has been provided not everyone will accept it. Therefore, the hope expressed by John in his pastoral concern will be realized only in those who come to Jesus Christ and by faith put their trust in Him for forgiveness and salvation.

SUMMARY (1:5 2:2)

John has a message to declare to his people, and it is a message of hope and enlightenment. He enlightens them concerning the nature of God by telling them that God is light and that there is no darkness in Him at all; no, not in any way. Those who walk in this light have fellowship with each other and with God, and their sins are being continuously cleansed as they walk. But those who only say that they walk in the light, but are really lying about their condition, are in darkness and have no truth in

38

them. There are some who are self-deceived about their sin-nature and their sin guiltiness. Some of them say they have no sinful nature and have therefore never sinned. These are only deceiving themselves and cannot perceive and understand the truth because of their self-deception. Some say that have never committed acts of sin, and thereby make God a liar who has said plainly in His word that everyone has sinned. These have rejected the Word of God by denying that they have ever committed sins. To those who confess their sinful natures and their acts of sin there is forgiveness and cleansing through the faithful work of Jesus Christ. The person and work of Jesus Christ is the means by which the sinner and the believer find forgiveness.

Although the ideal would be for the believer never to sin, the practical truth is that everyone sins. When the believer sins he has Jesus Christ to be his Advocate in pleading his case before the Father, and his Propitiation in taking his sins away. The forgiveness found in Christ and His sacrifice on the cross is for the whole world of people who have sinned and stand in need of forgiveness and salvation.

PRACTICAL TEACHING AND PREACHING APPLICATIONS (1:5-2:2)

There is so much wonderful truth here that can be practically applied to the hearts of all disciples of the Lord everywhere! Let us consider them one by one:

1. There can be an emphasis on the "Nature of God," or on a more down to earth theme, "Who is God, and What is God Like?" The

following points could be considered: A. He is a Holy God (1:5). He is absolutely LIGHT, and in Him there is no DARKNESS of any kind. Men need to understand that although God is holy He is still touched with the sinful condition of all men.

(A) He is a Hearing God (2:1), Jesus, Who is God wrapped in flesh, is our Advocate and pleads our case before the Father. Since it is Jesus doing the pleading, it is a certainty that the Father is HEARING these pleadings on behalf of the sinner. He is the same God who promised Jeremiah (33:3) that He would HEAR him and ANSWER him when he would "call upon him." Men need to know that God will HEAR them when they call upon Him for forgiveness and salvation.

(B) He is a Healing God (1:9). When·men come to Him, confessing their sins and by faith accepting Jesus Christ as their Saviour, God will not only forgive them, but He will CLEANSE them (purge, purify) of the disease of sin. He will be the HEALER of the sin malady which, if allowed to fester, could lead to eternal death. Men need to know that there is an alternative to death, and that alternative is life through faith in Jesus Christ.

2. There can also be a marvelous emphasis on SIN, for John says so much about it in these verses. Remembering that the word for sin used here is "hamartia," the most common word for sin in the New Testament, means "missing the mark" (Vine), we apply our teaching about sin from this passage thusly:

(A) The Calamity of Sin (1:8, 10). Sin causes a man to deceive himself (1:8) and to rebel against God to the point of total rejection of what God says (1:10). When a man is controlled by sin he is in effect under the control of Satan. That is the great calamity -the sinner will be what Satan wants him to be, and will eventually go where Satan is, to Hell!

(B) The Cure For Sin (1:9). Men need to know that there is a cure for their sin-that the malady does not have to be terminal. This cure for sin is to come to Christ and "confess" (say the same thing about sin that God does - agree with God about personal guilt) the sin that will destroy the sinner and receive from Christ forgiveness and cleansing.

(C) The Call for Sinners (2:2). Jesus is the Propitiation for the sins of the whole world, but only is individuals accept the offered salvation by faith. Jesus died for the whole world, and invites all men, no matter who they are, to come and receive from Him the forgiveness of their sins (John 3:16).

3. Another great application here is on FELLOWSHIP. John speaks about the fellowship that believers share with each other, and with the Father, and with the Son, Jesus Christ. This is a great emphasis for believers:

(A) This Fellowship is based on Truth (1:6). One cannot merely "claim" to share this fellowship in the Lord and with God's people. If one does not walk according to the teachings of the truth of God, they are liars and have no truth in them. Only those who have believed the truth and are living according to the truth can be a part of this fellowship. Therefore the basis of the fellowship is the truth of God. Men need to know there are some who may claim to be a part of the fellowship of God, but who are only liars because they do not accept or live by the truth of God.

(B) This Fellowship is born in Faith (1:7). The condition that John states in this verse is "if we walk in the light." To walk in the light of God requires faith in the Lord, and trust that He is LIGHT. When one places faith in Christ he steps into the LIGHT of God, and is therefore born into fellowship with the Father, the Son, and all other believers.

(C) This Fellowship Bears Fruit in Righteousness (1:7). The result, or the fruit, of waling in the light is that "the blood of Jesus Christ (keeps on cleansing) us from all sin." What a wonderful condition! To be constantly cleansed from sin as we walk in the light of God! Thus our fellowship with the Father, and the Son, and with other believers results in true righteousness through the blood of Jesus Christ.

4. The last of the practical truths to be emphasized here is concerning the Person and Work of Jesus Christ. Just as the nature of the Father is revealed in these verses, so the work of Jesus Christ is also revealed to us:

(A) It is the Work of Jesus to forget (1:9). He has said

He would forgive those who would come to Him confessing their sins, and He will. Men need to know that Jesus came to seek out those who would place their faith in Him (Luke 19:10) and that it is His desire and pleasure to forgive all, no matter who they are or what station in life they occupy, who will come to Him in faith.

(B)   It is the Work of Jesus to Plead (2:1).

John calls Jesus our ADVOCATE-one who comes along side of us to help us in our trouble - and an ADVOCATE is one who pleads for us before the Father. It is comforting to all who know the Lord Jesus to real that He sits at the right hand of the Father and pleads for us constantly.

(C)   It is the Work of Jesus to Atone for our sins (2:2).

John calls Jesus our PROPITIATION for sin. Through His sacrifice on the cross our sins have been taken away. This is the work of ATONEMENT. At last the sinner can be brought into perfect fellowship with God because his sins have been taken away and his guilt before God canceled.

B. By Obedience to God's Commands (2:3-11)

When the salvation which Jesus Christ provides for mankind is made effective by a personal and individual faith in Him, there is a change that comes into the life. This change is so striking and so complete that it is referred to as the "new birth" and John quotes Jesus in his Gospel account as saying, "Marvel not that I said unto thee, Ye must be born again," (John 3:7). This change brings to the believer a desire to follow the Lord Jesus and imitate His example. Following the Lord Jesus involves obedience to His commands, and an integral part of "Walking In the Light of God." If we obey His commands we identify ourselves as His "friends" (John 15:14).

(1) Our Obedience Reflected by Our Walk (vv.3-6)

"And hereby we do know that we know him, if we keep his commandments. "He that saith, I know him, and keepeth not his commandments, is a liar, and the truth is not in him.

"But whoso keepeth his word, in him verily is the love of God perfected: hereby we know that we are in him.
"He that saith he abideth in him ought himself also so to walk, even as he walked."

It is important that the believer have some evidence that he is a child of God and not just a pretender to faith. John addresses this need by saying in essence, "here is how we know that we are saved - here is how we know that we have a personal knowledge of God through the Lord Jesus Christ." It is a test which we can apply to our own lives. The test is obedience - not just servile obedience, but obedience which flows from a desire to please God, and from a heart which has been changed from wanting sinful things to one which desires those spiritual blessings which proceed from obeying the Lord in all things. Perhaps the key word concerning the commandments of the

Lord is the word "keep." It is used three times here in three different emphases:

(a) We know that we are saved, i.e. "know him," is we KEEP His commands - This emphasis is on the assurance to the believer that he is a believer. His life is now lived in complete obedience to the commands of His Lord and in imitation of the example of the Lord Jesus in all aspects of life. Assurance of salvation comes to one as he constantly seeks to obey the Lord in all things. Negatively speaking, this assurance fades and eventually disappears when the believer ceases to obey fully all that he knows God is commanding him.

(b) The person who only SAYS he is KEEPING the commands of the Lord and really fails to do so - this person does NOT know Him. He is a pretender to faith and not a possessor of Christ. He is not telling the truth about himself and his relationship to Christ, and because he is a deceiver the truth of God is not in him. It may be that the one described by John here was once faithful to the teachings of the Word, and one who understood the "truth" (that whole set of teachings about Christ and His Person and Work upon which we base our faith) enough that his life was changed, He walked in the light (1:7) and was blessed greatly of the Lord.

Perhaps something happened along the way and he began to slip back into the darkness, giving in to the temptations of Satan. Soon his was a life of deception, to himself (1:8) and to others. He joined the ranks of those who do not obey the truth, and thus became one in whom truth could not dwell. On the other hand, whoever KEEPS the Word, i.e. obeys the commands of the Lord, is one who is counted among the family of God. Two things are said about this person:

1. The love of God is "perfected." This word means "to bring to an end by completing" (Vine 174), or in plain language, to reach a goal. What is the goal of the love of God? To cleanse the believer so that he can enjoy perfect fellowship with God, "By his love God has brought him truly to know his God, truly to have fellowship with his God" (Lenski,408). The believer, then, reflects his cleansed and purified condition by obedience to the commands of the Lord.

2. The second product of KEEPING His commands is personal assurance that we know Him. This is a restatement of what is found in v. 3. We have assurance that we know the Lord Jesus when our lives are lived in complete obedience to the commands of the Lord.

The question remains - what are His commands? There are some who say that these are the moral commandments found in the Old Testament and that by obeying these commands one may know God apart from the "blood theology." That was the position of the Gnostics in John's day who sought to add knowledge to knowledge in order to know God. But one is not saved by obeying the moral commands, the Ten

Commandments, or even by adapting themselves to come kind of moral code of behavior.

Salvation comes through a Person, the Lord Jesus Christ, and His vicarious atonement, accomplished through His death on the cross. John has already said that in 1:7- "the BLOOD of Jesus Christ his Son cleanseth us from all sin."

The commands mentioned here are all the "words" (John 17:6-8) and all the teachings which Jesus delivered to those who followed Him by faith. "The substance ...consists of all the divine verities regarding God, and they produce actual fellowship with him in which we know him and know that we have known and know him" (Lenski, 405). It is all the "truth" in which we believe about Jesus, and which has changed our lives by its power.

Finally, John summarizes all that he has said in vv. 3-5 by saying in v. 6 that if we say we abide in Him we ought to walk like Him. It is said that the greatest form of flattery is imitation. It is also true that the most effective way the believer can bring glory to His Lord and attract others to Him is to imitate Him in all things. It is what we "ought" to do. Just as obedience is a proof of our knowing Christ, imitation is a proof of our spiritual identity with Him. We know Him, therefore we walk like Him, love like Him, obey like Him, and talk about Him to everyone we know.

(2) Our Obedience is Revealed by Our Love For Others {vv. 7-11)

a. Something New and Yet Old (vv. 7,8)

"Brethren, I write no new commandment unto you, but an old commandment which ye had from the beginning. The old commandment is the word which ye have heard from the beginning. "Again, a new commandment I write unto you, which thing is true in him and in you: because the darkness is past, and the true light now shineth."

John addresses his readers with the title "Brethren," revealing his deeply felt love for those to whom he was writing. Although he speaks with the authority of an apostle, he considers himself one among them. He has learned to speak the truth in love to those for whom he feels a great burden.   In other places in the epistle he refers to them as "beloved" (3:2, 21;4:1,7) and in doing so presents an example to all those who proclaim the truth to others of loving words and motives, These verses (vv. 7,8) would be a sort of preamble to what he would say to them in vv. 9-11 about loving one another, and he wants to set the scene by revealing his own personal love for them. In v. 7 he speaks of an "old commandment" which the people had from "the beginning."   There is a sense in which this "beginning" might refer to the Old Testament where the principle is plainly spelled out in Leviticus 19:18- " •.but thou shalt love thy neighbor as thyself •.n When Jesus was asked in the New Testament to identify the greatest commandment, He said that to "love thy neighbor as thyself" was the second most important commandment ever given to men (Matthew 22:34-40). The first was to "love the Lord thy God with all thine heart and that these two greatest commandments formed the basis of all the law and prophets. So then, when John spoke of love he spoke of a truth that the people should have already known because they had known it from the beginning.

There is another sense in which the "beginning might have referred to the beginning of John's ministry. In fact he says that this old commandment was the "word which they had heard from the beginning. Jesus taught the people with "words which revealed to them the heart of God, and brought new meaning to old truths. Jesus said, "A new commandment I give unto you. That ye love one another; as I have loved you, that ye also love one another" (John 13:34). So, from the very beginning of the proclaiming of the Gospel of salvation to men there existed the principle of loving one another.   This was old in that sense.

In v. 8 John changes the scene again by saying he was writing a "new commandment" to them, a new commandment that was really an old commandment as was discussed in v. 7. This old commandment had become new when Jesus came into the world proclaiming a new dimension of love to all men, and living in such a way as to reveal the way to love one another. The Gospel begins with the love of God expressed in the giving of Jesus to die for a world of sinful mankind (John 3:16) and continues in the example of Jesus going willingly to a cross to be the substitutional sacrifice for the sins of all men '(Romans 5:8).

As men believed in Him and imitated His life they, too, began to realize the truth of loving one another as He had loved.

The newness of this old truth "lies at the point of its realization and fulfillment" (Barker, 316).

In what way was this "old" commandment "new?"

It is a phenomena of human nature that a truth can be known in fact but the value of the truth can only become fully realized when its principle is demonstrated before our eyes. Jesus made the "old" commandment "new" not only by what He taught (John 13:34), but also by what He demonstrated to all men. For instance, Jesus came teaching that we ought to love our enemies and do them good and not evil (Luke 6:27-35). That was a hard pill to swallow for those who thought that enemies were those to whom all our animosity was to be vented.

Enemies were for destroying, not loving! Also, when Jesus proclaimed His Gospel of salvation, He said that it was for everyone, Jew and Gentile alike, and invited "all" to come to Him and accept His gift of salvation (Matthew 11:28). In these ways and many' more Jesus made the realization of the "new" commandment to be possible among men. "Love became new in Jesus because he widened its boundaries until there were none outside its embrace." (Barclay, 45).

This "thing" John speaks of is the new commandment to love one another. It is true in two ways: 1. It is true in Jesus because He has demonstrated by His life and ministry that He loved everyone to the point of complete self-sacrifice, 2. It is true in "you" (i.e. the believers who would read this epistle) because as the believer follows the Lord Jesus and becomes more and more like Him this principle of loving one another is more and more exemplified in daily living.

The reason why this principle of loving one another is true in Christ and progressively true in the believer is because "the darkness is past, and the true light now shineth." The darkness was the dim and recent past when Christ had not then been manifested in the flesh.

That was the time when men only knew the principle, the "old commandment, but not the exemplified truth in the Person of Jesus. Now the "light" is shining because Jesus has come and the darkness is gone because He has shown the world His light, the light of salvation and the light of a new relationship among men who now can love each other because He loved them first.

John refers to Jesus often as the "Light in the Gospel account. He begins by calling Him the true Light" (John 1:8), then quotes Jesus as saying that He was the "Light of the world" (John 8:12) and that all who followed Him would not "walk in darkness but would have the "light" of life, Jesus, then, is the Light that reveals to us not only the love of God in providing salvation for all men, but also the way all believers should live as they love each other in the way Jesus loved them.

b. The Test of Brotherly Love (vv. 9-11)

"He that saith he is in the light, and hateth his brother, is in darkness even until now.

He that loveth his brother abideth in the light, and there is none occasion of stumbling in him.

"But he that hateth his brother is in darkness, and walketh in darkness, and knoweth not whither he goeth, because the darkness hath blinded his eyes."

There no middle ground with John - one either loves or hates his brother. This love-hate test is applied to those claiming to be walking in the light of God, and the result of the test reveals the true believer. Lenski tends to believe that these three verses speak about three different kind of people:

1. The church member who has been deluded by those who hate and for whom there is some hope (v. 9), the true believer who demonstrates his true faith by the way he loves his brother (v. 10).

2. The one who has become a purposeful hater, who hates with purpose and seeks to destroy all those who claim to walk in the light (v. 11). This last one is ignorant of where he is going because the hatred in his heart has blinded his eyes to the realities of hell, for those who reject God and His love (Lenski, 414-416). Whether Lenski is right in his assessment or not, it is

obvious that John is speaking quite plainly here to the reality of a love-hate test to determine the genuineness of one's profession of faith in Jesus.

Verse 9 begins with another of those false claims we have encountered in this epistle before (1:6, 8, 10; 2:4). In this case it is one who is claiming to be in the light - that is, following Christ and walking according to His teachings - while at the same time manifesting a hatred toward his brother. John says of him that he is in "darkness" because of this false claim. One cannot follow Christ, Who teaches us that we ought to love one another, and continue to manifest hatred toward anyone. It is inconsistent with Christ's teachings, and, therefore, alien to being a true follower. John seems to hold out some hope for this one who is walking in darkness, for he says he does so "even until now." He is saying this one is in darkness up to and including this moment, but perhaps he will repent and come back to the light at some future time.

Which this may refer to another believer, but since the one hating cannot be included in this family because they are in "darkness," it is more likely that a general reference to all those with whom this person comes into contact is meant. Hatred can take many forms, and in order for us to make judgments about those who are in darkness, as John did, it is necessary to understand how one might hate his brother.

1. Hatred may take the form RESENTMENT- when one considers all others as unimportant, and elevates selfish

concerns to a position of importance above all others, then this form of hatred manifests itself. The market place is full of those who resent others constantly.

2.   Hatred may take the form of OPPORTUNISM - when people see others as only tools they can use to get ahead in business, or to get a favored position in society, they are called opportunists, and they manifest a form of hatred toward others. Hatred may take the form of ELITISM - when people treat others as their slaves, or consider all others on a lower social level than themselves, they are manifesting a form of hatred toward others.

3.   Hatred may take the form of ANIMOSITY - when people see others as their enemies and seek to oppose anything anyone else does simply because they do it, then they are manifesting a general animosity toward all fellow human beings which is blatant hatred.

This is why John says of those who hate their brothers that they are in "darkness." They are controlled by the powers of darkness and live in a constant state of guilt because of their hatred.

The contrast to this condition is revealed in v. 10 - here is the one who loves his brother, who manifests the very opposite of hatred toward those around him. Two things are said of this one who loves:

1. He abides in the light - that is, he walks according to the teachings of Jesus and in imitation of His example (1:7). His love for those around him is a living proof of the change that has taken place in his life since beginning to follow Jesus. The fact that he loves others is evidence that he has been changed from the self-centered sinner to the self-sacrificing believer.

2, Secondly, there is nothing in the lifestyle of the 'believer who is walking in the light that will cause others to "stumble."   There is nothing about him that will cause others to turn away from the truth of the Gospel and be lost.

The word translated "stumble" is the Greek "skandalon" which refers to a kind of trap to which bait is attached for the purpose of catching a prey. It is always used metaphorically in the New Testament and refers to anything that arouses prejudice, or becomes a hindrance to others, or causes them to fall by the way" (Vine, 129). Obviously this is not referring just too some missed step, but rather something as serious as to cause one to miss salvation in Jesus. Lenski says this means to bring "spiritual death" to others. (Lenski, 415). When the believer walks in the light, loving his brother, there is never anything in his life that would cause another to fail to gain heaven through faith in Christ.Just the opposite is true - the true believer will be living in such a way, and loving in such a way, as to attract others to Christ and to salvation in Him.

As if to emphasize again, with greater seriousness, the state of the one who hates his brother, John says of him that he does not know where he is going because he has been blinded by the darkness (v. 11). Everything about him is darkness (a synonym for sin) because he is walking in it daily, accumulating more and more guilt before God and manifesting more and more his hatred of others. His hatred has blinded him to the consequences of his sin.

He does not know that his way leads straight to Hell and the judgment of God. Jesus said that men did not know where they were going when they walked in darkness (John 12:35), and that, in fact, these who walked in darkness loved it because they thought it hid their wickedness (John 8:19). How sad the condition of those who walk so long in the darkness of sin that they become ignorant of the consequences of such an existence. The remedy is in Christ who said, "I am the light of the world: he that followeth me shall not walk in darkness, but shall have the light of life" (John 8:12).

SUMMARY (2:3-11)

This passage begins with a statement of assurance: "hereby do we know that we know him." (v. 3) and proceeds to apply two "tests to those claiming to know God, and giving assurance to those who pass the "tests that they are right with God.

The first test concerns obedience to the commands of God, and states plainly that anyone who claims to know God and does not live in obedience to the Lord's commandments is simply a liar. He is pretending to be something he is not, and therefore no truth can dwell in him. Lies are the very antithesis of truth, and the two cannot dwell in the same space. The one who is claiming that he knows God should walk in the same way as Jesus did, imitating His example in all things.

The second test concerns brotherly love, or our relationship to those around us. John states plainly that those who do not love others remain in the darkness of sin (v. 9) and have been blinded to what they are doing and where they are going (v. 11) by this darkness. On the other hand, those who love others prove by their love that they are walking in the light - conforming to the teachings of Jesus Christ and imitating His example in the matter of love - and they will never lead anyone into darkness because of their example. Rather, they will cause others to be attracted to the Lord because of their example of brotherly love.

PRACTICAL TEACHING AND PREACHING APPLICATIONS(2:3-11)

Even the most fundamental of truths needs application in order to be understood by those for whom it is intended. Jesus knew this when He taught in the Gospels using parables.

The parables He used were His way of making application of spiritual truth in order for His listeners to understand what He taught. In this passage we can find some wonderful applications of the truth contained herein:

1. The most obvious application here concerns the two tests" that are applied to determine if one is walking in the light - conforming to the teachings of Jesus and imitating His example. The outline of this lesson could be the following:

Title: THE TWO TESTS

Point A: The test of obedience (v. 4) - if a person is saying to others that he knows God, but is not obeying the commandments of the Lord - he is a liar! He has failed the test of obedience.

Point B: The test of brotherly love (v. 9) - if a person is saying that he is walking in the light but by his actions proves he hates those around him - he is really in the darkness and not the light.   He has failed the test of brotherly love!

Point C: The standard by which the test is applied (v. 6) those who say they know God should walk and act in the same way that He walked and acted. People who know the Lord imitate Him in all things! Only those who do so pass the test.

2. Another application can be made to the "perfecting" of God's love in the believer. The text verse is v. 5, "whoso keepeth his word, in him verily is the love of God perfected •." The word "perfected" means "completed, or fulfilled." The lesson here would be the following:

Title: LOVE PERFECTED

Point A: Love if perfected by obeying His word (v. 5) - Jesus obeyed His Father's will by coming into a sinful world and dying for sinful men. When we obey His Word we are imitating His obedience, and His love is completed, or fulfilled, in us.

Point B: Love is perfected by imitating Jesus' life (v. 6) - Those who have been cleansed of sin seek to imitate the Lord Jesus in all they do. By imitating Him (Christian means "little Christs") we perfect His love- bring it to a fulfillment.

Point C: Love is perfected by loving others (v. 10) - We are to love others in the same way and to the same extent that Jesus did.   In this way we bring God's love to its perfection, or completion - He loved us, we love Him, we love each other. This cycle requires the miracle of salvation to complete, for men's hearts have to be changed in order to love as Jesus loved.

3. The final emphasis here to be noted is that of "FOLLOWING THE LIGHT" as pointed out in v. 8- "The darkness is past, and the true light now shineth." This "true light" is the Lord Jesus Christ Whose life and sacrifice on the cross has given new meaning to an old commandment to "love thy neighbor as thyself" (Leviticus 19:18). As believers we should follow the "true light" and imitate His example because:

(A) There is no DARKNESS (sin) in this Light (v. 9) - no one will ever be led to sin by following Jesus, · for there is no possibility of sin in Him. Rather, as we follow Him we become more and more like Him and therefore less likely to sin.

(B) There is no DANGER of stumbling in this Light (v. 10) - to cause to "stumble" means to hinder someone from finding salvation. When we walk in imitation of Jesus there will never be anything in our lives that would cause someone else to lose their way, or fail to find salvation in Christ.

(C) There is no DISASTROUS END in following this Light (v. 11) - Those who walk in darkness - live in sin and live according to the dictates of Satan - are ignorant of where they are going.

They do not know that to follow darkness is to walk blindly, and that this blind walk leads straight to Hell. Those who follow Jesus will never come to such a disastrous end, but rather will find life everlasting in Heaven with Him.

C. By Avoiding Involvement With The World System (2:12-17)

Continuing his pastoral concern for those for whom he has a special burden, John expresses his desire that they not become entangled with the secular world system that surrounds.

He has great confidence in these believers, as is expressed in his loving appeal to them, but he also recognizes the allurement of the secular world system, and the dangers of falling into its trap. These verses reveal to us not only the loving concern of John, but also his practical realization of the dangers that threaten every true child of God.

1. A Loving Appeal (vv. 12-14)

John prefaces his warning about the world system with loving words of encouragement to the people and their leaders.

This appeal is in a sort of poetic form, expressed in two stanzas to the same people.

(a) First Stanza (vv. 12-13b)

"I write unto you, little children, because your sins are forgiven you for his name's sake.

"I write unto you, fathers, because ye have known him that is from the beginning. I write unto you, young men, because ye have overcome the wicked one.

As we read this loving appeal to the believers we must bear in mind that what John says will precede his warning about the secular world system. He is saying by this appeal that he has confidence in them and knows that their past victories will enable them to face the threat of the world system and keep them from becoming entangled in it.

This appeal is very positive from John's point of view, and reflects how he feels about the spiritual maturity of the people.

The appeal is addressed to three groups of believers: the "little children," the fathers and the young men. This is not to be thought of as singling out different age groups in the church, but rather to think of it as an address to the whole church represented by the mature believers and those who are comparatively young in the faith. "Little children" is a term which. John uses to address the church as a whole.

In this epistle he uses it in 2:1,28; 3:7; 4:4; 5:21; in each case referring to the whole congregation. There is a little difference in the words here translated "little children." In v. 12 it is the Greek "teknia" which refers to a child young in age; while in v. 13c it is the Greek "paidia" which refers to a child young in experience and in need of instruction. (Barclay, 51}.

"Fathers represent those who are mature in the faith and able to instruct others, while "young men" represents those who have more recently found the Saviour and the forgiveness of their sins. In each case John gives a reason why he is writing to them, and each reason is encouraging:

1.   He writes to the "little children" (i.e., the whole congregation of believers) because their sins are forgiven. That is why they are the little children - they are a part of the family of God and therefore not only under John's pastoral care, but also are the children of God and under His protection and guidance as well.

2.   He writes to the "fathers" because they have "known him that is from the beginning." These were the more mature male members of the congregation who had for some time walked in the light of God, and thus were able to pass on their mature wisdom and understanding to those younger in the faith than they.

These must " hand the torch of the Gospel light to the next generation, namely the young men in the church." (Kistemaker, 267).

3. He writes to the "young men" in the church because they had "overcome the wicked one."They have withstood the onslaught of temptation and placed their faith in the Lord Jesus Christ for cleansing, forgiveness, and strength to keep on staying true.   In essence John is saying, in an encouraging way, to these young men, "You made the wisest decision in your life - now keep true to the commitment you have made. More temptation is coming, but I have confidence in you that you will win the victory!" The young in faith need this kind of constant encouragement to help them grow stronger and stronger in the Lord.

(b) The Second Stanza (vv. 13-14)

"I write into you, little children, because ye have known the Father.

"I have written unto you, fathers, because ye have known

him that is from the beginning. I have written unto you, young men, because ye are strong, and the word of God abideth in you, and ye have overcome the wicked one."

The second stanza of this appeal is almost identical to the first, with some exception. The same people are addresses, although there is the distinction mentioned earlier as to the word translated "little children." There is no doubt that the same meaning attaches here, that is, he is speaking to the whole congregation of believers. There is a little difference in the messages of the appeal.

1. In this stanza John writes to the "little children" because they have "known the Father." They came to know the Father when their sins were forgiven, as mentioned in v. 12, "for his name's sake." This is simply saying that these believers have come to experience the love of the Father through the Lord Jesus Christ, through whom they found the forgiveness of sins. It is precisely this truth that will help them to reject the appeal of the secular world system when they are confronted with its temptations. There can be no more glorious experience in the world than to know the Father" and all the love He extends to those who walk in His light.

2. He writes to the "Fathers" in this second stanza with the very same appeal he used in the first stanza. The meaning has not changed, but the repetition of the appeal gives us some idea of the seriousness of the matter with which John will deal in his warning about the world system.

3.   He writes to the "young men" for two additional reasons: because they are "strong" and because the word of God "abideth in you." They had already proven their strength by "overcoming the wicked one" and choosing to follow the Lord Jesus. The means by which they had overcome the wicked one was the Word of God - unless this Word was in them they would have never been able to overcome. These young men would be the hope of the future of the church. John wanted to encourage them to maintain their integrity by continuing in the faith which they had been taught. They would need their strength for the days ahead when the world system would seek to lead them away from the Lord and from their spiritual victory already won.

(3) The Plague of the Secular World System (vv. 15-17)

"Love not the world, neither the things that are in the world. If sins were forgiven, as mentioned in v. 12, "for his name's sake." This is simply saying that these believers have come to experience the love of the Father through the Lord Jesus Christ, through whom they found the forgiveness of sins. It is precisely this truth that will help them to reject the appeal of the secular world system when they are confronted with its temptations. There can be no more glorious experience in the world than to "know the Father" and all the love He extends to those who walk in His light.

He is speaking to believers here, for there is no reason to appeal to the unbeliever who has already succumbed to the corruptness of the world system and has been captivated by it.

John's concern is for the believer, who through weakness of the flesh and the strong appeal of the world system, might drift away from his relationship with the Lord Jesus Christ.

"Love not the world, neither the things that are in the world. If any man love the world, the love of the Father is not in him.

"For all that is in the world, the lust of the flesh, and the lust of the eyes, and the pride of life, is not of the Father, but is of the world.

"And the world passeth away, and the lust thereof: but he that doeth the will of God abideth forever."

John uses the strongest word for love here when, he says "Love not the world." The word is "agape" which "indicates direction of the will and intelligent, purposeful choice ..." (Lenski, 423). His appeal to the believer is to not allow the things that are in the world to turn his attention away from faith in the Lord Jesus. One cannot be in love with the world and also in love with the Father.   James says in his epistle that the believer cannot even be a "friend" (Greek "phileo," a word of lesser intensity than "agape") to the world because to do so would mean that he had become an enemy of God (James 4:4). Loving the world is the antithesis of loving the Father, and the two cannot be in agreement at all.

The question naturally follows, what is the world? Even though the word translated world here is the Greek "cosmos," it is not being used to describe the created world. There is nothing at all wrong with the world which God has created. It is full of beauty and is a reflection of God's love for all mankind because in it He has placed everything that man needs to maintain life. John cannot mean the created world, but must be using the word to describe something entirely different. In the Gospel of John he said that God loved the world (John 3:16), and there he was referring to the world of mankind. God loves all men, no matter what state they are in spiritually. God's love to mankind is unconditional and extended to all men everywhere. So then, the "world" cannot mean the created world nor can it mean mankind in general.

The "world" as John is using it here refers to a corrupt world system which has come to oppose the influence of Christ on earth. (Lenski, 423). H.A. Ironside calls it "that system that man has built up in this scene, in which he is trying to make himself happy without God." (Ironside, 73). It is a world system that rejected any influence of God and has gone about to establish a world order based on man's abilities and intellect.

Because man is basically corrupt and depraved, the world which he has attempted to manufacture for himself is also corrupt, and is in opposition to God in every respect.

This is the world which the believer must resist with all his might, because this is the world which will ridicule the believer's faith and belittle his experience with the Lord, and in the long run has the potential for destroying the relationship that brings life and the promise of an eternity in heaven.

There are two reasons offered why the believer must reject the world system.

(1)He must reject it because loving the world leaves no room for the love of the Father.   It is not that the Father does not love him, but that the love of the world has become so strong and so ell-encompassing that there is no room for the Father's love in the heart which has become enamored of the world system.

(2) He must reject the world system because it is a dying system (v. 17). This corrupt system is under the judgment of God and even now is moving toward total destruction. Barker calls it a "corpse not yet buried" (Barker, 322) and he is absolutely correct. So then, because loving the world precludes loving the Father, and because the world is dying and soon will "pass away" entirely, the believer must reject all allurements from the world system that would attempt to draw him away from the Father's love.

In v. 16 John categorizes "all that is in the world" under three headings. In v. 15 he mentioned the "things that are in the world" and here he draws the attention of the believer to the specifics of those "things."

(1) First, there is the "lust of the flesh." The "flesh" is the "sphere of our fallen and sinful nature" (Stott, 100) and refers to that outlook which is oriented toward self and is occupied with pursuing its own interests in a "self-sufficient independence of God," (Barker, 321). It can be said that this "lust" begins within, for the depraved nature of man always seeks to make itself known, and opposes any effort to deny its desires. This is that desire for self-gratification which so characterizes this age, and which weakens the ability to commit to anything, much less God. It affects relationships (marriage, friendship, etc.) by destroying them. The one who seeks self-gratification cannot GIVE anything to a relationship because they are only seeking to GET something out of it. It affects the religious life of the nation, because people are only interested in what they can GET out of the church, rather than what they can GIVE in worship and service to the Lord.

(2) Secondly, there is the "lust of the eyes" which refers to those allurements of the world system which originate from without. It includes everything that entices the eyes, the things that one might look upon with longing and desire.

One of the classic examples of this kind of desire is David's sin with Bathsheba (2 Samuel 11). He first looked upon her beauty, then desired her, then took her in an act of adultery that led to great sadness and loss of joy in David's life (Psalm 51:12).

(3) There is much in this world to appeal to the "eyes" and the believer must be careful to resist them. Included among them are the allurements to sexual sins that abound everywhere.

There is no lack of "eye appeal" to such sins in literature, in the entertainment presented on television, in movies, and in the material world.

(4)   Thirdly, there is the "pride of life." This is the most difficult of the three to define because it speaks in such a general way. The primary word translated as the "pride of life" is the Greek "alazoneia" which refers to a "pretentious hypocrite who glories in himself or in his possessions" (Barker, 322). The word itself is defined as "hollow, vainglorious pretense" (Lenski, 426).

One who spends his life glorifying all that he has, or all that he does, is said to be an "egotist."   Some of the old-timers had it right when they described one like that as being "full of himself." That is exactly what this "pride of life" is - it is being "full of one's self" and occupied totally with ambition, possessions, and self-interest. It is that ugly manifestation of character which is illustrated in the "me first" attitude so prevalent in the world. It is illustrated by those who will cut another's throat to get ahead in business, or cheat others to make a profit, or lie to get ahead. It is the distorted values of a materialistic culture which measures everything in terms of cost or how much pleasure it will bring to the individual. The believer makes a mistake when these "things that are in the world are thought of as being unattractive and unappealing.

When one assumes that John speaks only of the ugly things in the world there is the danger of falling for the allurements that are not so unattractive. Even the beautiful things of this world can defeat the believer if care is not taken to avoid their dominance in the life. Music, good literature, education, recreation, etc., are all good and can be a source of satisfaction to the believer - that is, until they become the dominant interest in the life. When the believer loves anything in this world so much that his love for the Father is diminished, at that point he has succumbed to the world system and is in need of sincere repentance and forgiveness. Remember, all that is in the world - the lust of the flesh (allurements which originate from within), the lust of the eyes (allurements which originate from without), and the pride of life (the desire for position and respect within the world system) - is not "of" (literally, "out of") the Father, but is "of" ("out of") the world system, and therefore must be avoided by the believer. Finally, John draws attention to the choice that believers must consciously make. Remember that "love" is defined as an "intelligent, purposeful choice" (Lenski, 423) and therefore is under the control of the individual. The choice the believer has is outlined in v. 17 as between the world system that is passing away, and even now has the stink of death upon it, and doing the will of God which has the breath of life in it.

It is a choice between life and death, between heaven and hell, between joy and despair.

SUMMARY (2:12-17}

With an attitude of loving concern John addresses the believer about the progress that has been made spiritually in their lives. His tender feelings for them is revealed by the words he uses to begin his remarks. He calls them "little children," and sounds like a father speaking to his special little ones. He commends the Fathers for their maturity in the faith and for their steadfastness in knowing "him that is from the beginning." The young men are commended for their strength and for their ability to overcome the wicked one in their lives. Obviously the ministry of John had borne fruit in the lives of those who were a part of the whole congregation.

After commending these believers for their progress in the Christian life, John warns them about the threats to their relationship with the Lord Jesus.　He calls upon them to be extremely careful about the corrupt world system in which they lived, because that system would attempt to destroy them. He calls upon them to avoid falling in love with the world through the allurements offered through the desires of the flesh, the eyes, and the pretentiousness of the pride of life.

These are all things that belong to the corrupt world system and not to God. The world system is already in its death throes, and those who fall in love with will also die with it. There is no life in the world; only death.　The choice is obvious: give in to the appeal of the world system and die with it, or do the will of God and share in the rewards of the faithful forever. Doing the will of God brings life - life that is eternal and filled with the blessings of the Lord.

PRACTICAL TEACHING AND PREACHING APPLICATION (2:12-17)

The teacher or the preacher will have no trouble finding life applications here in these verses! There is a storehouse of truth that can be applied to modern day Christian experience. For instance, every preacher will want to learn from John how to maintain a loving relationship with those in his congregation. We see in vv. 12-14 how John encourages his people and speaks positively about the progress they have made in the Christian li. He recognizes, as we all must, that people need reinforcement about their Christian life, and that by simple encouragement we help them along their spiritual pathway - a pathway made more difficult because they live in a corrupt world. Who needs this encouragement? The Fathers (older, more mature believers) need it because the journey has been long and sometimes they grow tired along the way. The young men (new converts, not long in the faith and therefore less mature and knowledgeable about spiritual things) need encouragement because they need to be founded upon the truth of the Word. The whole family needs encouragement because they face daily the threats that come from the world system that would seek to destroy their faith. Preachers and teachers need to learn how to be "encouragers" rather than "critics" of the people to whom they minister.

In v. 14 the message to the young men concerns their strength and how they have overcome the wicked one. A great lesson could be taught here about the "Strength That Prevails." Three points could be emphasized here:

(1) The SOURCE of that strength lies in a personal relationship with the Lord Jesus Christ. These young men had recently trusted in the Lord Jesus and He had brought them to victory. The victory was not in their own abilities or talents, but in the Person of the Lord Jesus and His might.

(2) The SUSTAINING of that strength lies in the Word of God. John said of these young men that the "word of God abideth in you." As they digested the Word in their hearts and lives the strength came that enabled them to oppose the corruptness they found in the world. The Word becomes to all believers the source of being sustained in the midst of a very wicked world. There we discover the will of God, and there we discover the love of God as He expresses it day by day,

(3) The SURMOUNTING POWER of that strength results in overcoming the wicked one in this world. Every believer must have this power, for the way is hard at times and the danger is great. With the power and strength of God flowing through us as a result of our relationship with Christ, and our knowledge of the Word, there is no threat to our faith that cannot be met and overcome!

Another emphasis, so needed in this very wicked time in history, is that of the danger of the world system to the believer.

Remember that John's words were written to believers, not to sinners. His concern was for those who already had placed their faith in the Lord Jesus Christ that they would be contaminated by the world around them. The subject could be: "How To Avoid The Dangers of Life."

The following practical points could be emphasized:

(1) Don't give in to the appeal of the depraved nature in each of us. Remember that all of us are afflicted with a sinful nature, and sometimes that nature will call for us to give in to the sin around us and become a part of it. Don't allow your sinful nature to take control of your life. Remember, "...Greater is he that is in you, than he that is in the world" (4:4).

{2} Don't allow your vision to be dimmed by the allurements around you. Your eyes will the gate through which the devil will attempt to get at your heart, but ask God for the strength to close your eyes to the sinful things which appeal to the flesh and which appear beautiful to the eyes. Keep looking to Jesus and allow all your vision to be taken up with Him.

(3) Lose all interest in what others think of you. Don't be worried about what others say about you - be more concerned about what God thinks of you. Instead of seeking to please self, lift up the Lord and put Him first in your life and do not become consumed with the desire to be recognized by this sinful world. Such recognition is fleeting at best, for the world is passing away. The recognition the believer needs is that which comes from God Himself - this recognition will abide forever!

D. By Rejecting the Teaching of the Antichrists (2:18-28)

The word antichrist is found only in the epistles of John and nowhere else in the New Testament, but the concept is found in Paul's mention of the "man of sin" in 2 Thessalonians 2:3,4 and the mention of the beast" in Revelation 13:1; 16:13; 19:20; and 20:10, and in several passages in the Old Testament.

In this passage he calls upon believers to reject the teaching of the antichrists who are already in the world if they are to remain true to the teaching of the Lord Jesus Christ.

Who are these antichrists? The word comes from the Greek "antichristos" which can mean either (1) opposed to Christ, or (2) instead of, or seeking to replace Christ (Vine, 61). In the first meaning the description is one of a blatant opposition to Christ, open and vocal in putting down the teachings of Christ.

It is this kind of opposition that is the easiest for the believer to resist because it so blatant, and therefore unquestionably opposed to Christ. The second, however is much more subtle because it implies that there is opposition from within - hidden because it may pretend to be a part of the believing congregation. The believer will have a difficult time defending against such an influence because it is hidden and therefore dangerous in its ability to deceive and destroy.

It is possible that the meaning here is a combination of the two - that there was both an open and blatant opposition to the teachings of Jesus Christ, and that there was also a hidden influence from within the church that pretended to be a part of the congregation but was in reality seeking to destroy the effectiveness of Christian teaching. It is more likely that this meaning will be the more accurate one as we look at what John says about the danger of the threat of the antichrists.

Simply stated the concept of the antichrist as proposed by John is this: just as Christ is the incarnation of God and goodness, so the antichrist is the incarnation of the devil and evil.

Over the years many have made the attempt to identify this antichrist by name, calling such men as Antiochus Epiphanes, Nero, Hitler, Stalin, and others "the" antichrist - the one single individual in some period of history who seems to be the incarnation of all that is evil.

Paul seems to give some support to this in 2 Thessalonians 2:3,4 as he describes the "man of sin" who will exalt himself above all that is called God and cause men to worship him rather than God. But John's description seems to imply not so much a single individual as being "the" antichrist, but a principle espoused by many individuals that seeks to destroy the faith of the true believer. He calls this the "spirit of antichrist" in 4:3.

The warning, then, that John is presenting to the believer is a warning against the principle of the antichrist, "the principle which is actively opposed to God in any generation, incarnating itself in those who blatantly oppose God'1   (Barclay, 63). This principle will be present in all generations and even then was present in the world and presenting a threat to those believers for whom John was concerned.

1. The warning about the   any antichrists (:1, 19)

"Little children, it is the last time: and as ye have heard that antichrist shall come, even now are there many antichrists; whereby we know that it is the last time.

"They went out from us, but they were not of us; for if they had been of us, they would no doubt have continued with us: but they went out, that they might be made manifest that they were not all of us."

John warns the believers that the "last times" (literally - "last hour") have come, and that the signal of these last times was the fact that the antichrist would make an appearance.

He says not only has the antichrist made his appearance, but that "many" antichrists were already in the world.

To John, and to all believers in that generation, the new age had dawned when the Messiah came into the world. When Jesus was crucified on the cross and then rose again, the hope and faith of all Christians had been established. When He ascended the angel said that He would come again "in like manner as ye have seen him go into heaven" (Acts 1:11). The expectation of all believers in that generation was for the immediate return of the Lord Jesus Christ to this earth. It becomes obvious as one reads through the New Testament that Christians thought of themselves as living in "the last days" just prior to that return of Jesus Christ to this earth. John had an anticipation of the return of Christ as being at any time, and thus to him, as it should be with all of us in this generation, the "last hour" was every hour he lived (Barclay, 60}.

One of the signs of this "last hour" preceding the coming of the Lord was the deception of many false prophets and the cooling of the love of many believers (Matthew 24:10-13).

When the antichrists began to depart from among the believers John felt sure that the end was near for all that was wicked and deceptive, and that soon Jesus would return to set things right. Thus he says that the way to know that the last times had come was that there were many antichrists in the world.

In v. 19 we find out that these antichrists were once a part of the church membership. John says, "They went out from us, but they were not of us"   They were those in the church who opposed the work of the Gospel, perhaps even openly hindering at times what the church tried to accomplish for the glory of God.

Perhaps these even tried to; overcome the leadership of the church and created confusion and disagreement within the local body of believers. They shared a membership in the church but not an agreement with the teachings of Christ in every respect. As Stott so aptly describes them, "They share our earthly company, but not our heavenly birth" (Stott, 106}.

Because these antichrists failed in their attempt to take over the church from within, they left of their own volition- "they went out" - and began another phase of their deception, an opposition from without the church.

There is little doubt in most minds that John is referring to the Gnostics who so opposed his ministry, and who taught such deceptions of the Gospel that many were influenced by them and left the faith of Jesus Christ. Although they left of their own who they were. Counterfeit believers cannot remain so for very long when in the presence of other true believers. As Paul taught in 1 Corinthians 3:13, "Every man's work shall be made manifest" and he mentioned two sources of that revealing: the "day shall declare it (that is, the day of the coming of the Lord Jesus when all men shall be judged righteously) and the fire" shall reveal it (the fire of God's judgment).

He further mentions in 1 Corinthians 4:5 that when Jesus comes all the hidden things will be made manifest.

These counterfeit believers revealed themselves by their works, and soon left the fellowship of true believers because there was nothing commonly shared among them about the teachings of Jesus Christ.

Had they been truly a part of the shared faith of the true believer they would have stayed with them and not departed, but because they were believers in name only they departed.

There was a Divine intention accomplished by the departure of the antichrists.They departed so that "they might be made manifest that they were not all of us."

The Divine intention was that these false believers might be revealed for what they were - counterfeits! If they had been true believers they would have stayed with the congregation, but since they were not, they departed. "Those who are of us stay with us. Future and final perseverance is the ultimate test of a past participation in Christ" (Stott, 105).

John's warning is clear: there are many antichrists in the world and they are revealed by the fact they have departed from among the faithful and are now openly opposing· the teachings of Jesus Christ. His warning to the believers of that generation is as up to date as this morning's newspaper, for there are antichrists in the world now, (and they are openly and actively opposing everything that God stands for, and seek to hinder the Gospel that Jesus proclaimed through the church then, and is seeking to proclaim through the true church today.

2.   The antichrists are liars (2:20-23)

But ye have an unction from the Holy One, and ye know all things. "I have not written unto you because ye know not the truth, but because ye know it, and that no lie is of the truth.

"Who is a liar but he that denieth that Jesus is the Christ? He is antichrist that denieth the Father and the Son.

"Whosoever denieth the Son, the same hath not the Father: but he that acknowledgeth the Son hath the Father also."

That John did not have in mind the true believers in the congregation is reflected in his statement of confidence in v. 20.

He believed that the true believer had an "unction" from the Holy One and therefore was able to discern the difference between truth and error. The word translated "unction" is the Greek word "chrisman which is translated anointing" in 2:27.

This is a reference to the effect of anointing and not to the act of anointing. The fact that the believers had received an unction from the Holy One n •• indicates that their anointing renders them holy, separating them to God" (Vine, 59). This anointing came from the "Holy One" Whom Lenski equates with Christ (Lenski, 435) and Whom Barnes equates with the Holy Spirit (Barnes, 1477). A very interesting progression is proposed by Lenski in the following way: the Anointed One - Christ (christos) gives His anointing (chrisma) to the true believer, uniting the believer to Him as His anointed (christoi) and thus presenting a contrast to those who have joined with the antichrists and are identified with total opposition to God and the teachings of Christ (Lenski, 434).

The idea presented here is that the believer is one with Christ because of the anointing, and thus inbred with certain knowledge that is a protection from the antichrists.

John says that as a result of the anointing the true believer "knows all things." This is not to infer that true believers have some unusual capacity for knowing the things of science, art, history, etc.; but rather that they have been given the ability to know the truth about the difference between that which is false and that which is true.

When confronting the Pharisees in the Gospel of John Jesus said, "If ye continue in my word, then are ye my disciples indeed; and ye shall know the truth, and the truth shall make you free." Jesus implied here that not only would believers be made "free" from the guilt of their sins by believing on Him, but that they also would know the truth which would make them able to resist the error with which they would be confronted.

So then, when John says that these believers "know all things" he means that they know all that they need to know about the truth of God in order to recognize a lie when they hear or see it.

In v. 21 John continues to Show his personal confidence in his fellow believers by saying that he had not written to them to inform them about the truth; he had written to them because they already knew the truth, and thus could act on that truth by rejecting the error of the antichrists.

The basic truth that they already know is that "no lie is of the truth." A lie and the truth are in opposition to each other and have no ground for agreement. The knowledge of the truth possessed by every true believer is the ground for defense against the lies of the opposition as represented by the antichrists.   This knowledge would enable the true believer to reject the deceptive teaching of the antichrists and remain true to the Lord Jesus.

In verses 22 and 23 John presents the means by which the antichrists can be tested. The antichrists are liars because they deny, that Jesus is the Christ (Anointed One), the Messiah promised in the Old Testament.

This denial took the form of the teaching of the Gnostics of John's day. Cerinthus, one of the major teachers of this heresy, developed the idea of an "Eon Christ" who had his home in heaven.   This "Eon Christ" descended from heaven and occupied the body of Jesus at His baptism, but left His body just prior to His crucifixion, thus effectively denying the Son and the efficacy of the blood of Jesus for the sins of all men (1:7), This philosophy was a denial of Jesus as the Christ (Lenski, 437).

This lie propagated by the Gnostics effectively denied the teachings of Jesus, and threatened the faith of the true believer by its deception. They were admitting to Jesus being the vessel of the spirit of Christ during His lifetime, but denying that in the flesh He was the Messiah, A half-truth is more dangerous than a lie in any generation, and John was fearful that some of the true believers might be tricked into believing this half-truth, which was not truth at all, but a lie.

We are reminded of some of those today who teach that Jesus was a "good man" and a "great teacher" but would deny His deity. They are proclaiming the same lie that John warned against here. The more things change, the more that stay the same. True believers are fighting the same battles that John fought, only today it seems that the spirit of the antichrists win more often than they lose! V. 23 states the fact that to deny the Son - that is to deny that Jesus is the Son of God in the flesh, not just possessing the spirit of the "Eon Christ" - is also to deny the Father, because the Father sent the Son and the Father and Son are equal (John 3:16; 10:30).

One cannot have one without the other. If a person claims to know the Father, but denies .what the Father has taught and rejects whom .the Father sends, he really does not know the Father.

He has rejected the Father by rejecting the Son. Here is seen the exclusivity of the Gospel of Jesus Christ - that is, that no religion that rejects Jesus Christ can possess the approval or the Person of the Father.To leave Jesus out of the faith of any religion is to negate that faith - it is an empty and meaningless faith that denies the Son.

The latter part of verse 23 appears in italics in the King James Version, indicating that these words were added by the translators. These words do not appear in many MSS, but they do appear in others. Barnes indicates they do appear in the following MSS: the Vulgate, the Syriac, the Ethiopic, the Coptic, the Armenian, and the Arabic versions. The words also appear in the critical editions of Griesbach, Tittman, and Hahn. (Barnes, 1478). The intent of the latter part of the verse is clear. It is to express the same idea in the first part of the verse: To deny the Son is effectively to deny the Father; but to acknowledge the Son is to also acknowledge the Father.

Thus the character of the antichrists as being liars is effectively outlined by John.They are liars because they deny the truth about Jesus Christ, and since they deny the truth about Jesus Christ they also have denied the Father as well.

They are liars when they say they have the Father while all the time denying the Son. True believers, because of their anointing from the Holy One, are able to recognize this error and thus reject it out of hand.

3. The antichrists are seducers (2:24-26)

"Let that therefore abide in you, which ye have heard from the beginning. If that which ye have heard from the beginning shall remain in you, ye also shall continue in the Son, and in the Father.

"And this is the promise that he hath promised us, even eternal life.

"These things have I written unto you concerning them that seduce you."

Not only are the antichrists liars in their denial of Jesus as the Son of God, the Messiah Who has come to redeem man from his sins, but they are not content until they have been able to "seduce" others to their way of thinking. In v. 26 John says that he is writing these things to warn against those who would "seduce" the true believer. To "seduce" means "to cause to wander, to lead astray" (Vine, 336), and the antichrists' intention as far as John was concerned was to lead the true believer away from the faith that he had been taught from the beginning of the ministry of John.

This danger of seduction is why John encourages the true believers to stay true to the things they had heard "from the beginning." The beginning refers to the beginnings of John's ministry to them, and is a way of saying to these believers, "Keep on believing what you heard in the beginning. The Gospel has not changed, the apostolic teaching has not changed, and even though the antichrists would have you believe that it has."

The word "abide" here means to "continue, and most certainly infers a continuance without interruption (Vine, 10}.

The encouragement concerning these first teachings is to "let" them abide. The fact is that these things would not automatically remain in the hearts of the believers themselves, the teachings must be allowed to remain there by the believers themselves. There must be a willingness to allow the truths of the Gospel to remain in the heart for them to remain there, and any rejection of them in part or whole will mean that they will not remain. The fact is that believers can be deceived (3:7), and all believers must make every effort to resist such deception so that they can remain true to the Lord.

To remain true to the teaching received from the beginning would mean that the believer would also continue in fellowship with the Father and with the Son. "The Apostolic testimony is directed essentially to the Son That is why it will keep them true to Him if they remain true to it" (Stott, 113).

One of the signs of the "perilous times" spoken of by the Apostle Paul was that some would not "endure sound doctrine" but would rather seek teachers that would please them in the flesh (2 Timothy 4:3). To remain in these teachings from the beginning would be a source of defense against the error that would always seek to "seduce" the true believer. The promise given to those so remaining is eternal life (v. 25).

This is a life beyond this one, a life filled with that perfect fellowship with the Father and the Son found only in heaven, Thus the threat of the antichrists is not only for this life, but also is a threat that could rob the true believer of eternal life.

The effort should be made at all costs to resist the error taught by the antichrists, for to give in to their deception would mean the loss of Divine fellowship here and also in the -life to

Commentary on the Epistle of FIRST JOHN

come.

4. The safe-guard against the antichrists (2:27, 28)

But the anointing which ye have received of him abideth in you, and ye need not that any man teach you: but as the same anointing teacheth you of all things, and is truth, and is no lie, and even as it hath taught you, ye shall abide in him.

"And now, little children, abide in him; that, when he shall appear, we may have confidence, and not be ashamed before him at his coming."

John again refers to the anointing which the true believer has received (v. 20), and says that this anointing "abides" or remains in them. This was not a transient experience, but one that would continue to remain in them as long as they allowed it to remain (v. 24).

Because they had experienced this anointing there was no need for others to teach them - others such as the Gnostics who claimed to have some special insight about God and about Jesus Christ. They could trust the anointing that they had received because:

1.   This anointing continued to teach them all things. Again the "all things" does not imply some great ability to understand all secular facts, but refers to everything that they needed to know in order to remain in the Lord Jesus Christ. The

Holy Spirit is the Teacher that maintains a continual ministry of teaching to the true believer so that he always has the knowledge necessary to reject false teaching.

2.   This anointing was true - not counterfeit as all of the teaching of the antichrists was. "The test of the anointing was its fidelity to that which was from the beginning" (Barker, 327).

There are those who try to proclaim that there is "new revelation" for this day and they are always speaking those things which they claim come from God. Always remember that God will not contradict Himself in anything that He has already said. A test of the reliability of all spiritual teaching is its adherence to the truths first proclaimed by the apostles and the Lord Jesus Christ.

3.   3. This anointing had already brought forth fruit in these believers, as John said, "even as it hath taught you." This is a reference to the past experience the believers had in the teaching of Christ.   The fruit produced by it was pure and fed their souls.   Past experience gives confidence for present loyalty on the part of the believers. Because of the effects of the anointing they had received, John had utmost confidence that these believers would remain faithful to the Lord Jesus and not give in to the influence of the antichrists. They would continue to "abide" in Him, and thus not become victims to the erroneous teaching with which they would be bombarded. In v. 28 John again encourages the believers to "abide" in the Lord Jesus. The reason given here is that they would have "confidence" and not

be "ashamed" at His coming.

The word that is translated "coming" is from the Greek "parousia" which describes a joyful event. In secular usage it described the festivities that attended the arrival of a monarch on a state visit. These would be joyful events, filled with music and laughter. (Barker, 328). By John's usage of the word he implied that the coming of Christ would be a joyful event for the true believer. That joy would be marred if he was ashamed for some reason. John says that shame can be avoided if the believer continues to abide in the Lord Jesus Christ. Instead of shame there would be "confidence" in the heart of the believer. Lenski calls this "the undismayed confidence of faith." (Lenski, 444).
When faith is present there is no need to be ashamed; only a sense of anticipation at His coming. This is an event that all believers should look forward to with great joy. Thus, the great defense of the believer against all the error of the antichrists is that anointing of the Holy Spirit in the life which teaches the believer all he needs to know in order to remain true to the Lord.

If he remains true to the Lord there will not be any reason to be ashamed when Jesus returns to claim His own, but rather a wonderful rejoicing at His appearing.

SUMMARY {2:18-28)

The pastor's heart that characterized John's ministry and this epistle is seen clearly in this section about the antichrist.

He is concerned about the believers under his care, and seeks to warn them about the presence in the world of many antichrists - those who oppose not only the work of Christ in the world, but who also seek to confuse and destroy those who believe in the Lord Jesus Christ. John indicates that many of these antichrists were once numbered among the congregation, but since they were not truly sharing the same faith as other believers they soon departed from among them.

Their departing was an indication of their true identity.

The nature of these antichrists is that of deception - they are liars! They have denied that the Son is the Christ that has come in the flesh, and by denying and rejecting Him they have also denied the Father. This is the false doctrine that they would have the true believer to accept, and by accepting it become apostate to the true faith of Jesus Christ.

Every believer, however, has an anointing from God which will enable them to reject totally this error, and by rejecting the error maintain their true faith and salvation in Jesus Christ.

Since these antichrists will use every device at their command to seduce the true believer away from the true faith, the believers are encouraged to stay true to the Gospel they had heard "from the beginning."

If the teaching they heard from John, and others, remains in them they will not depart from the faith and be shipwrecked spiritually.   Rather, they would continue in the fellowship they enjoyed with each other, and with the Father and the Son.

They would also have the anointing of God - the Holy Spirit - as their teacher and sustainer through any difficult time of opposition from the antichrists. By maintaining this faith and rejecting the influence of the antichrists they would be able to stand before the Lord with confidence at His coming.

The believer ought to be able to anticipate with joy the appearing of the Lord Jesus Christ, and he can if he allows the ministry of the Holy Spirit to teach him all he needs to know to be protected against the influence of those who would seek to destroy him.   John here seeks to prepare his fellow believers for the coming of the Lord by showing them the reality of the antichrists in the world, and by showing them how to reject their influence and stay true to the Lord Jesus.

PRACTICAL PREACHING AND TEACHING APPLICATIONS (2:18-28)

If a warning against the antichrists was so needed in the days of John, the danger has certainly increased in our age to the point that a warning is a vital necessity for the spiritual health of all believers.

The first application here concerns the identity of the enemy: could title the lesson "KNOW THINE ENEMY" In the passage we can point out the characteristics of the antichrists as a way of helping the believer to recognize the enemy:

(1) THE ENEMY GOES OUT FROM THE CONGREGATION (v. 19). They are uncomfortable in the congregation because they are not in agreement with the faith of the members of the congregation. They may appear in form for a while to be a part of the family of believers, but all the while they reject the Saviour and His sacrifice for the sins of all men.

These are "counterfeit Christians who will, sooner or later, leave the fellowship pf true believers and join the ranks of those who oppose all that is godly and righteous. We may know that they are of the antichrist when they depart from among the true believers and embrace an opposing doctrine that is not consistent with the teaching of the Word.

(2) THE ENEMY LIES ABOUT THE PERSON OF JESUS CHRIST (vv. 22, 23). They refuse to accept the truth about the Son which John has taught and which the Scriptures teach that Jesus Christ is God's Son, wrapped in flesh and walking among men. They may teach that Jesus is just a good man, or a good teacher, but that we need not deify Him by making Him equal with the Father.

Their lies may take the form of logic, philosophy, ridicule, etc. - anything that can be used to confuse the minds and hearts of believers.   But all they teach is a lie, because they teach those things that are in opposition to revealed truth. The believer must always remember that all doctrine must be tested against what the Word of God says, and anything that is in disagreement with the Word will always be a lie.

(3) THE ENEMY WILL SEEK TO SEDUCE THE BELIEVER (v. 26).   Sometimes a lie will be rejected out of hand by those with even a casual acquaintance with the Word. But when the enemy uses seduction the danger becomes greater.

Seduction works because it will appeal to the basic nature of man: the need for recognition, flattery, and acceptance by others.

Even a lie presented in these frameworks will become believable because the victim sincerely desires to believe it.

A part of the success of modern day cults is not so much in their effectiveness at promulgating a lie, but in their ability to create a desire in people for their teaching, For instance, the Mormons use an appeal to family life and traditional moral values to entice many to embrace their group.   Only after they are firmly established in the group are they indoctrinated with the false teachings of the Mormon religion.

A follow up on a message about knowing the enemy would be an emphasis on "HOW TO RESIST THE ANTICHRISTS IN THE WORLD" - this would be a positive message to strengthen the believer who is exposed daily to the enticements of the influence of the antichrists. Believers need the encouragement of fellow believers and the faithful teaching of the Word to be able to successfully resist the forces that surround them daily and that seek to destroy their faith.

{1} WE RESIST THE ANTICHRIST BY ALLOWING THE HOLY SPIRIT TO STRENGTHEN US (v. 20). Human effort and ingenuity are not enough to do spiritual battle with the forces of evil in this world. If we try to do battle with our own strength we will surely fail. But the believer has an "unction" - an anointing - from the Holy One.

It is this anointing in the person of the Holy Spirit that will spell the difference between success and failure in the battle.

The believer will have all the knowledge necessary to resist the forts of the antichrists in the world by simply relying on the Person of the Holy Spirit to strengthen and sustain him.

(2) WE RESIST THE ANTICHRIST BY REAFFIRMING OUR FAITH IN THE TEACHINGS OF THE GOSPEL (v. 24). Those things which we heard in the beginning of our salvation - those things which first stirred the faith that brought us to Christ - are still powerful enough to keep us in the Lord and away from the forces of evil in this world. We do not find this strength in the

teachings of philosophy, sociology, psychology, and other sciences. We find the strength in a simple faith and acceptance of all that Jesus taught in the Gospels. The principles of confession of sin, repentance, and trust in the atoning work of the Saviour may sound simplistic to those seeking refuge from the fury of the enemy, but they still work, and by employing them the "peace that passeth understanding" is brought to the believer's heart.

(3) WE RESIST THE ANTICHRIST BY ABIDING IN CHRIST (v. 28). The sense that abiding in Him" has here is that of remaining and resting in the teachings of Christ, structuring our lives by this teaching, and rejecting the false teaching that surrounds us every day.

By so abiding in Him there will be nothing of which we need to be ashamed when He shall appear in His coming, when our hearts are filled with the Lord Jesus Christ we need not fear the efforts of the antichrists to seduce us or make us believe a lie. Those who abide in Christ are always safe from the enemy.

II. EXPERIENCING THE RIGHTEOUSNESS OF GOD (2:29-4:6)

Now we move into a new dimension of John's exhortation to his flock, and we include ourselves as being the objects of his exhortation. He moves from speaking about the "fellowship" that all believers share in the Lord Jesus Christ - walking in the light of Christ, obeying the commands of Christ, knowing the world system for what it is, evil and wicked, and purposely rejecting the seduction of the many antichrists that are in the world - to the dimension of the personal experience of the righteousness of Christ, that righteousness which He possesses as the Son of God, and that righteousness which he bestows upon all that place their faith in Him as personal Saviour and Lord. Righteousness as applied to the Lord Jesus Christ has the sense that He is right or just and has done right in the way He has dealt with sin on behalf of all men (Vine, 298).

Righteousness as applied to those who have accepted Jesus Christ as personal Saviour has the sense that through Him believers have been brought into right relation with God, a relationship which is unattainable through any other means except through Him (1 Corinthians 5:21). It is John's concern and burden that all believers truly experience this righteousness to its fullest degree, and be blessed by the experience.

A.   By Knowing Christ, Who is the Righteousness of Believers (2:29-3:10)

1.   The Mark of Righteousness (2:29)

"If ye know that he is righteous, ye know that every one that doeth righteousness is born of him."

John has already told his readers that God is righteous in 1:9 where he indicates that God does right in forgiving the believer of sin when confession is made. He has also indicated that Jesus Christ is righteous in 2:1 in that He does the right thing for believers by serving as their Advocate before the Father.

To whom, then, is John referring by the pronoun "he?" We understand who this is by the phrase "born of him." In every case in this epistle this is used to indicate God {3:1, 9; 4:7; 5:18), since we are always born of God and not Christ. Christ is the Divine instrument by whom we are born of God.

He is the One who pays our penalty for sin and makes it possib1e for the believer to be forgiven and made new, i.e. "born again."So then, the Person referred to in this verse is most certainly God the Father.

"If ye know" refers to a knowledge to which the believer has come through faith and the instruction of the Word.

The word "know" appears twice in this verse, the first time being derived from the Greek "eidate" (Berry, 610) which has the sense of perceiving, or understanding the real meaning of something. This understanding can come either from Divine knowledge or from observation of the thing or person to be understood (Vine, 298). This word must be in connection with the second "know" which comes from the Greek ginosko."

The idea here is that if the believer has come to a full perception of the person of God the Father as being righteous, then he also will make progress in understanding that those who imitate Him in His righteousness are "born of Him."

The chief fact that the believer has come to perceive is that God the Father is righteous. This knowledge has come from two sources, as the meaning of the Greek word indicates: from Divine revelation and from the believer's own observation of the Father's works among men. Righteousness is an absolute attribute of the Father - He can be no less than absolutely righteous. If He were anything less than righteous He would not be God!

As a result of the believer coming to the full perception and understanding of the righteousness of God, there is planted in the heart a desire to imitate Him in doing the same kind of righteousness that God does.

This imitating of the righteousness of God in the life of the believer is the identifying "mark" that he has been born of Him.

This righteousness of the believer's part is the 1'perceptible evidence of our birth" (Lenski, 447).

This is not just claiming righteousness by some act of supposed goodness to others; this is righteousness that has been brought about by a "new birth" in the believer (2 Corinthians 5:17). The believer does righteousness because he has been made righteous by the blood of Jesus Christ.   All he does has declared righteous because he seeks to please God in everything he does.

The one who is claiming a self-righteousness is doing so under false pretenses because simple human morality does not constitute relation to God the Father. That relationship can come about only through the blood of Jesus (1:7,9; 2:3-5).

2. The Hope of Righteousness (3:1-3)

"Behold, what manner of love the Father hath bestowed upon us, that we should be called the sons of God: therefore the world knoweth us not, because it knew him not.

"Beloved, now are we the sons of God, and it doth not yet appear what we shall be: but we know that, when he shall appear, we shall be like him; for we shall see him as he is.

"And every man that hath this hope in him purifieth himself, even as he is pure.

In these three verses we see three things about the believer as he experiences the righteousness of God: (1) we see what the believer is now - a son of God; (2) we see what the believer shall be as a result of this son ship - like Him; and (3) we see what the believer does as a result of this hope - he purifies himself.

The believer experiences the righteousness of God not only by doing righteousness (2:29), but also by being declared "sons of God." This declaration is the cause of John's outburst here of great astonishment, "Behold." He has just indicated in 2:29 that the believer is born of God 'and therefore is characterized by God's righteousness. But it is amazing to

John that believers should now be called the "sons of God."

There is a sense in which every living creature owes its existence to the creative power of God, for God has created everything that is in the world. But being created by God does not necessarily mean that one shares a "family" relationship to Him.   This family relationship comes about as a result of faith in Christ and the resulting cleansing of sin in the life of the believer.

Once that cleansing has taken place by the Divine miracle of salvation, God declares that the believer is His son (literally a "child") and that God is his Father.

John is amazed that God's love would go so far. He says, "what manner of love" the Father has given. The word "manner" is from the Greek "potapen" (Berry, 611) which refers to the country of origin of someone (Vine, 38), or of what sort someone is.

John seems to be amazed at the love that God has bestowed, wondering where such love came from, or of what sort it is.

Certainly it is a love that did not and cannot originate in the heart of finite man. It most certainly is a love that comes from Heaven itself, from the heart of an infinite God who is capable of loving beyond the ability of man.   When salvation comes to the heart of the believer he is related to God not only by virtue of the fact of creation, but also by virtue of the fact that he has been declared a "son of God," a member of the Divine family. What a holy relationship, and to be recognized by the Father Himself as one of His children!

As a result of this Divine relationship, the world does not know or understand the children of God. The reason for this is plainly stated - because the world did not know or understand Him (referring certainly to Christ, Who was rejected of men when He came into the world).

The world of unsaved men and women find it impossible to understand the faith of the believer - a faith that motivates him to sacrificial service and a pure lifestyle. The world will never understand the believer because it never understood Jesus Christ. Their eyes were blinded by their purposeful rejection and their spiritual ignorance.

The believer is so different as a result of the change which Jesus has effected in the believer (2 Corinthians 5:17) that the world stands and scratches its head at the sight of the redeemed living for Christ here and looking forward to the appearing of Jesus Christ one day.

The second verse opens with John's favorite address to those who are the objects of his ministry. He· calls the believer "Beloved" because he loves each one, and also because he has just reminded the believer that God loves him, too. God's infinite and glorious love has made it possible for believers to be the "sons of God" - related by blood and by the New Birth. That is the present condition of all truly born again believers.

That present condition is fully realized because we have the witness of the Word of God and the experience of the presence of the indwelling Holy Spirit (Romans 8:16). It is a glorious condition because of the fellowship we share with each other and with the Father and the Son (1:3,7).

The only real mystery is "what we shall be." It is a mystery because we have not yet experienced it, so then, it "doth not yet appear" to the believer.

Perhaps the reason why it does not presently appear to the believer is because in this life all of us still are faced with having to deal with the infirmities of the flesh with all that implies. Here the believer sees only the dark side of existence, but that will soon be overshadowed with the wonderful, awesome, and glorious presence of the Lord Himself! What does appear is the certain hope that the believer will be "like him" (Christ) because He will at last be seen in His total reality, "as he is."

If the believer is to be "like him" there must be a change that takes place to enable that which is of the flesh to be fasioned into something spiritual and thus deserving of such a divine inheritance. Paul speaks of this change in Philippians 3:20,21, when he says that the believer will be changed, "that it (the body) may be fashioned like unto his glorious body".

Thus, in the day in which Christ shall appear the true believers will cease their humiliation of having to live in such a "vile body" and be made into a likeness of the body and existence of Christ Himself! What a grand expectation! What a wonderful hope!

Now, all who have this hope (v. 3) will be in a continual process of purifying themselves. Those who have stopped this process of purification no longer have fellowship with Him (1:6), and thus have no real hope. But those who look forward to the day when they shall be like Him, and shall go through a complete metamorphosis of exchanging this vile body for a glorious body like His, will be always seeking to become more and more like Him (2:29), doing righteousness as they know to do it, and avoiding the sin that can and will corrupt their lives.

The standard by which the believer determines how far he should go in this process of purification is Christ Himself.

We are to look to Jesus for our pattern and example of righteousness, and seek to be as pure as He is. This is not an impossible task, for Christ is not only our example and pattern for this righteousness, but He is also our enabler, making it possible for all believers to be "made the righteousness of God in him" (2 Corin. 5:21). So the process of purification is really a process of walking with the Lord Jesus, maintaining our faith in Him, and trusting Him always for forgiveness and righteousness. That is what John meant when he said in 1:7- "if we walk in the light, as he is in the light, we have fellowship one with another, and the blood of Jesus Christ his Son cleanseth us from all sin."

3. The Test of Righteousness (3:4-6)

"Whosoever committeth sin transgresseth also the law: for sin is a transgression of the law."

"And ye know that he was manifested to take away our sins; and in him is no sin.

"Whosoever abideth in him sinneth not: whosoever sinneth hath not seen him, neither known him,"

There is a wonderful progression here being expressed by John. It is full of logic as well as spiritual truth. Note the three points that he is making: (1) Those who sin are transgressors of the law; (2) Jesus was manifested to take away our sins; (3) Those who are characterized by continual sinning do not know Christ.

This is the test of true righteousness, and the test of whether or not a person is a true believer. It is a simple test: If your life is characterized by continual sinning, you do not know Christ - you are NOT a true believer! The reason is that Christ has paid the price to take away the sin of believers, not only the guilt of sin but the inclination toward sinning, and those who know Him are constantly seeking to be like Him (3:3). This test is to be applied by all believers to those who make false claims about their relationship to Christ, and to themselves to determine if their faith us genuine or not.

The word "transgression" in v. 4 refers to a "lawlessness" (Vine, 149) in those who sin. That is, those who sin do not feel that they are subject to the law, and therefore not bound by it. They have decided that they are a law unto themselves, and are not willing to bring themselves under the restrictions of the law of God. It is a form of rebellion against all that is godly and holy, and especially a rebellion against God Himself! John is not only making a statement about all those whose lives are characterized by sinning, he is also defining for us what sin is - it is a rejection of all law, and especially the law of God.

One gets the sense here of "sin out of control," even the control of the sinner himself! If there is no law which the sinner respects, and no law to which he owes any submission, then he is under the control of the master sinner, the devil himself, The sinner has rejected the Lordship of Christ, and made himself the servant of the devil (Romans 6:16)!

John turns to what should be the greatest source of encouragement to all men, especially to those who have, by their rebellion against God, become the slaves of sin. There is a way out of that slavery, a way to be released from all the dominion of sin forever (Romans 6:12-14)! How is this to be done? Through Christ, for "he was manifested to take away our sins.   (v. 5). John made this proclamation in his Gospel account when he said of Jesus who had come to be baptized of him, "Behold the Lamb of God, which taketh away the sins of the world" (John 1:29}. No man has to live under the slavery of sin any longer, because Jesus has come to make it possible for all to be forgiven of all their sins, and for all men, women, and children in the world to go free from this awful domination. That was why He came to live among men - to take our sin away and to give to all who would take it "everlasting life" (John 3:16).

What is it that qualifies Jesus to take away the sin of the sinner? It is because "in him is no sin" (v. 5b).By His sinlessness He is qualified to be the "Lamb of God," the sacrificial offering for the sins of all men everywhere. He is God's Lamb in the sense that God gave Him (John 3:16), and also in the sense that there could be no other source for such forgiveness and salvation. When we speak of the sinlessness of Jesus we mean that there is nothing at all in Him that is tended to commit sin, and that there has never been a sin committed by Him at all! Only such a sinless One is qualified to be the offering for the sins of all men.

Finally, John moves to his conclusion in this logical order of things. In verse 6 he says two things of great importance: (1) that those who abide in Christ do not continue in sin, and (2) that those who do continue in sin do not know Him, neither have they ever truly seen Him as who He is - the Saviour of men, the One who can take their sins away.

As to the first of the facts John states: "Whosoever abideth in him sinneth not a very simple and straightforward statement. There are really two verbs that concern us here.

The first is the word "abideth." The simple meaning is to continue" (Vine, 10). So then, to "abide" in Christ is to continue" in him, without pause or reservation. Those who do not continue in Christ are those who have allowed sin to become dominant again in their lives, but those who are continuing in the Lord are those who have purified themselves and are not characterized by constant sinning.

The second word is "sinneth. The word here comes from "hamartia" which refers to missing the mark" and is in the form of continual action. Therefore, what John is saying is that one who continues in Christ will NOT continue in sin - sin will NOT characterize his life. This does not mean that the believer is sinlessly perfect, but rather that he will constantly make the effort to purify himself (3:3), and that when he weakens and sins he will seek forgiveness (1:7). Only Christ is perfectly sinless, and it is not within the realm of possibility for any person who is in the flesh to become so. It is only as we place our faith in the sinless Christ that God considers the believer as being righteous and without the guilt of sin. Paul, the great Apostle, speaks of this conflict within himself• in Romans 7:14-25 and refers to the fact that there is that weakness concerning sin in him, and if in him, then in all believers.

The proof remains, however, that those who are continuing in Christ do not allow sin to dominate their lives, nor do they allow sin to characterize them at all. Conversely, those who do allow such sinning in their lives, who make no effort at purification and righteousness, but become characterized by sinning - these are not, neither can they be in any way called, true believers. It is precisely because of their habit of sinning, rebelling against the law of God (3:4), that they can claim no kinship with Christ. John has already said that such a person who may claim to know Christ but continues to disobey His commandments is a "liar, and the truth is not in him" (2:4). He has not "seen" him because he suffers from spiritual blindness caused by the darkness in which he abides {2:11).

The knowledge referred to here when John says that this person has not "known him" is a knowledge that goes beyond intellectual comprehension to the point that it produces a spiritual effect in the person (Lenski, 459).

Since the one continuing in sin has evidenced that he has not seen Christ, it is also evident that he has not come to the knowledge that would produce a spiritual regeneration.

So then, the test is applied accurately. Since sin is an act of lawlessness and rejection of God, and since Jesus was manifested to take away such lawlessness, then those who are true believers are those who have rejected lawlessness and are making the effort to purify themselves constantly through the blood of Christ. The false professors can be known by the fact that they are continually sinning and making no effort at righteousness and purity.

4. The Warning About Deception (3:7-10)

"Little children, let no man deceive you: he that doeth righteousness is righteous, even as he is righteous.

"He that committeth sin is of the devil; for the devil sinneth from the beginning. For this; purpose the Son of God was manifested, that he might destroy the works of the devil.

"Whosoever is born of God doth not commit sin; for his seed remaineth in him: and he cannot sin, because he is born of God.
"In this the children of God are manifest, and the children of the devil: whosoever doeth not righteousness is not of God, neither he that loveth not his brother."

John reduces the test of determining whether or not a person is a true believer down to its basic form:

(1) Righteousness is of God therefore those who do righteousness belong to God;

(2) Sin is of the devil - therefore those whose lives are characterized by sin belong to the devil. There can be no clearer test in the mind of John, and he desires that this same clarity will be realized in the minds and hearts of his readers.

He is genuinely concerned that they not be deceived by those who would corrupt the difference between the true believer and those who only pretend to be true believers.

This difference between the true believer and those pretending to be so has been corrupted in every generation, and in this present generation it has taken on new importance.

In the minds of many there is little difference at all. The idea is that so long as a person is "religious" there should be no effort to determine the true believer. Even the word "Christian" means something entirely different than it did when first conceived. Then it meant that one was a disciple of Jesus Christ and was attempting to live in the manner of Jesus Himself.

These disciples were so "Christ-like" in their behavior that the secular world called them "Christians." Today the word "Christian" may mean any of a long list of things, and many things called "Christian" have nothing at all to do with Jesus Christ.

Surely the deception is taking place everywhere, making the instruction of John concerning the difference between the true believer and the pretenders of this world more vital than ever.

In verse 7 John again addresses his readers with the loving title "little children." His Pastor's heart goes out to them because he is concerned about the deception that was even then in the world, and he considers them as his own "children" because they had come to know the Saviour through his ministry.

He then proceeds to the primary reason for vv. 7-10 - he says, "Let no man deceive you."   Notice first the SOURCE of any such deception - it from man. The Good News of the Gospel and the gift of salvation came from God in the person of Jesus Christ. Jesus was the "WAY, the TRUTH, and the LIFE" (John 14:6). He did not just tell the truth - He was TRUTH personified - He WAS truth! So then, the TRUTH was of God - but deception, which is a lie and the antithesis of the truth, originates with man. The danger to the believer lies not in the truth of God, but in the deception of man.

The believers to whom John was writing were surrounded by religions of all sorts, which proclaimed so-called truth in very loud voices. They lived in an environment which would make it easy for even the most sincere of believers to become confused as to what was real and what was fake. False prophets abound in our age, and many sincere believers are often deceived by their half-truths and convincing words. It is dangerous to automatically discount the possibility of becoming deceived by the falseness that surrounds believers every day. Paul's admonition to the Corinthians is still applicable today: "Wherefore let him that thinketh he standeth take heed lest he fall" (1 Corinthians 10:12).

Now to the meat of what John was teaching. The positive side of this warning concerned how to tell who was a true believer. To John it was simple, "he that doeth righteousness is righteous" The extent of this righteousness was according to the pattern of Jesus Himself: "even as he (Jesus) is righteous."

The "doing" of righteousness proceeds from a heart that has been made righteous in the sight of God through the process of the New Birth. Sinful man in his natural state is not capable of righteousness, and therefore must be changed from within.

This miraculous change occurs through the power of Grace working in his heart. "Righteousness" refers to the character of being right or just (Vine, 298) and "righteous" refers to the condition of a person who is in harmony with the holiness of God (Vine, 298). This harmony with the holiness of God will find expression outwardly in the believer's condemnation of sin in all its forms.

Like the refreshing waters from an artesian spring flow naturally from deep within the earth, so righteousness flows from the life of one who has been cleansed from within and made holy by the blood of Jesus Christ (2 Corinthians 5:21).

The writer of Proverbs said it best when he said, For as he thinketh in his heart, so is he" (Proverbs 23:7).

The sense here is that the believer is acting from the heart that has been made like God's heart. This heart is full of love, compassion, and just dealing with those with whom the believer comes in contact. The standard is God's righteousness expressed in the person of Jesus Christ. This changed heart is the product of the action of the Holy Spirit - it is called the "fruit of the Spirit" - and is expressed by "love, joy, peace, longsuffering, gentleness, goodness, faith, meekness, temperance." (Galatians 5:22, 23). No one should be deceived about this absolute requirement of those who are true believers – if one is a true believer he is acting from a heart made like to God's heart and is characterized by righteous acts of justice and mercy. Conversely, if one claims to be a true believer and is not characterized by such righteousness, his claim is false.

His attempt at deception can be countered by a simple examination of his life and attitudes.

Negatively, John addresses the warning about those whose lives are characterized by sin. In v. 8 he says plainly that those who commit sin are of the devil, because the devil has been sinning from the very beginning. The devil represents all that is wicked and depraved, and those who live like the devil are of the devil. They may speak swelling words that sound religious, but if their lives are patterned after everything that is wicked and wrong they are not of God - THEY ARE OF THE DEVIL!

The sense is the same in both the positive picture presented of those "doing righteousness" and those "doing the sin." In both cases we are speaking to what characterizes both kinds of people, the true saint and the sinner (Lenski, 460).

John is saying that the believer who consistently does righteousness is revealing that he is of God, while the one who consistently sins, and is characterized by this sin, is revealing that he is of the devil.

It does not mean that the true believer NEVER sins, nor that the sinner does not occasionally do some work of righteousness (in the sense of doing justly in his relationships to others). The fact is that believers often sin through ignorance or spiritual weakness, and when such sin occurs the remedy must be applied according to the formula which John has already revealed in 1:9 and 2:1. But this sinning on the part of the believer, if he is a true believer, creates a sense of guilt with which he cannot long endure. He is not characterized by this sinning, and he is not comfortable with the guilt of it, and thus he runs to the cross and finds forgiveness and cleansing. The difference between this true believer and the sinner is that the sinner is not characterized by occasional acts of righteousness, but by his constant sinning and failure to feel any guilt about his sinning. It is the consistent characterization of either sin or righteousness that determines for the observer what lies in the heart of the person. Although no one can truly know another's heart except God, a person's conduct and attitude is usually a good indicator of what kind of character he has, John's compassionate heart is again revealed in the next statement. While he stated clearly the difference between the true believer and the sinner, his Pastor's heart wanted those who were under the deception of Satan to be freed of that deception. Consequently he reminds his readers that "the Son of God was manifested, that he might destroy the works of the devil" {v. 8b}.

The work of the devil is a work of deception and spiritual destruction, He seeks to devour all whom he can (1 Peter 5:8) and is characterized as the "adversary" of all men.

One who has been so deceived does not have to remain under the devil's spell, for Jesus came for the express purpose of destroying the works of the devil. Jesus thwarted the efforts of Satan to capture the souls of men everywhere by paying the penalty of sin in His own blood on the cross. Now a man does not have to die in his sins, but can be delivered from them and have eternal life {John 3:16). If one who hears the Gospel in all its clarity and simplicity dies without being forgiven it is because he made the choice between being deceived by Satan and being saved by the grace of God.

SOURCES USED BY AUTHOR:

The author had already passed away before this publication-and no Bibliography was found. I have added those writers from whom he researched and am not sure the edition or publisher he may have used.

Kistemaker, Simon J. New Testament Commentary - James, Epistles of John, Peter, and Jude. Publisher: Baker Books (January 1996)

Lenski, Richard C. H., a native of Germany, was educated in the United States at Capital University, Columbus,Ohio, where he served as a professor and seminary dean, along with his several pastoral appointments in Ohio. Interpretation of the I & II Epistles of Peter the Three Epistles of John and the Epistle of Jude..

Thiessen, Henry C. Lectures in Systematic Theology. Publisher: Eerdmans, William B. publishing (January 1, 1975)

Robert G. Gromacki (Th.D., Grace Theological Seminary) is distinguished professor emeritus of Bible and Greek at Cedarville University in Cedarville, Ohio. New Testament Survey: Publisher: Baker Academic. Publication Date: May 31, 1974

TDNT Theological Dictionary of the New Testament. Publisher: Wm. B. Eerdmans Publishing Co.; 10th edition (August 1, 1984)

John R. W. Stott (1921-2011) has been known worldwide as a preacher, evangelist and communicator of Scripture. For many years he served as rector of All Souls Church in London, His book is unknown since the author passed before this printing.

W.E. Vine, M.A., was a classical scholar, skilled expositor, and a trustworthy theologian. Recognized internationally for his outstanding Greek scholarship, his *Expository Dictionary of New Testament Words*, first published in 1939, represents the fruit of his lifetime labors and is an unsurpassed classic in its field. --This text refers to an out of print or unavailable edition of this title.

Harry A. Ironside: Addresses on the Epistles of John
(Ironside Commentary Series). Numerous publishers.

Glenn Barker, Writer and Editor of Word Biblical Commentary.

William Barclay (1907-1978), Professor of Divinity at the University of Glasgow, and wrote more than fifty books--most of which are still in print today.

www.ingramcontent.com/pod-product-compliance
Lightning Source LLC
Chambersburg PA
CBHW061746020426
42331CB00006B/1372